Tangles with Pike

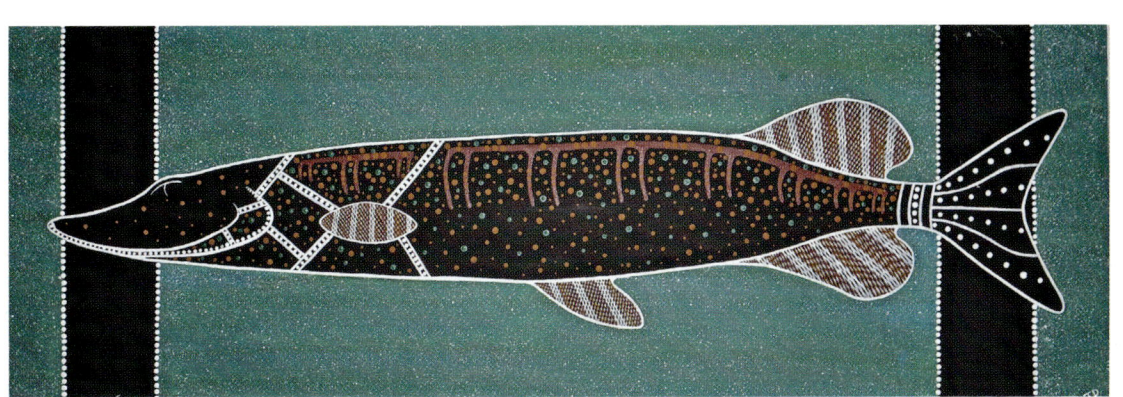

DOMINIC GARNETT

Tangles with Pike

Copyright © 2014 Dominic Garnett. All rights reserved.
First paperback edition printed 2014 in the United Kingdom
A catalogue record for this book is available from the British Library.

ISBN 978-0-9931204-0-4

No part of this book shall be reproduced or transmitted in any form or by any means, electronic or mechanical, including photocopying, recording, or by any information retrieval system without written permission of the publisher.

Published by DG Fishing
For more copies of this book, go to: www.dgfishing.co.uk

Designed and Set by Fisherman Creative Ltd

Printed in Great Britain by The Printing House
London www.theprintinghouseuk.com

Cover illustration: Copyright © David Miller 2014. www.davidmillerart.co.uk

Title page art by John Dullaway.
www.johndullaway.com (signed prints available at www.dgfishing.co.uk)

Although every precaution has been taken in the preparation of this book, the publisher and author assume no responsibility for errors or omissions. Neither is any liability assumed for damages resulting from the use of this information contained herein.

Contents:

4	FOREWORD
6	A TALE OF TWO HALVES
8	IN THE CLEAR
16	LOST IN SOMERSET
24	REINVENTING A LOST ART
32	THE MONSTER AND THE JERK
38	OF ICE AND MEN
42	THE PROFESSOR AND THE PIKE
50	CHEWED OFF
56	MURDER BY NIGHT
60	THE UGLY DUCKLING
64	REVENGE ON THE WYE
70	TARRANT VS. TEETH
78	PIKE FISHING IN SUSPENSE
84	ESOX AND THE CITY
92	ADVENTURES IN LAKELAND
102	THE OPPORTUNIST PIKER
112	RIVER PIKE IN THE ROUGH
118	WHERE THERE'S MUCK...
122	THE USUAL SUSPECT?

Foreword

Non-anglers often like to imagine fishing as a "relaxing" pastime, but feelings of peace and tranquility are not always those that evoke my most vivid experiences of pike fishing. The sudden pop of a bright float, the curious burning feeling of fingers numb with cold, the wild rush of a hooked fish—these are the sensations of the pike angler.

I have been lucky enough to catch some fine pike, but it is the thrill of the experience that grabs me beyond the pounds and ounces. Hence the chapters in this collection are those I hope succeeded in telling a decent yarn or evoking a little of the magic and excitement of pike fishing, rather than the usual "here are a load of big fish and here's how I caught them." That said, you'll certainly find the odd monster and articles that might give you some fresh ideas to incorporate into your own angling.

It has been a long and sometimes steep road for me with both words and fishing, but pike have always inspired my writing. *Esox Lucius* was the catalyst for my first ever published fishing article, "Reinventing a Lost Art", which can be found on page 24. In between you'll find all sorts of topics from close encounters with pike in clear waters, to experiments using unconventional rigs, flies and even home made imitations of water rats and ducklings. You'll also find some very different angles on pike, such as travels to the far north of Europe and days on the bank with some of the real characters I've enjoyed fishing with.

This anthology encompasses highlights from various sources. Several articles are favourites from the past decade, others are new or previously unpublished. Some parts have been clipped here and there, whereas in other places the more outlandish or outspoken parts have been left in their original form rather than cropped. You won't find all my writing here, but certainly

those pieces I felt were worth celebrating and enjoying again. After all, it is the secret pain of the angling hack that even his best crafted pieces often last just a week or at most one month.

Make of these stories what you will then. No doubt pike anglers certainly will, being an opinionated lot! Whether or not you catch more pike as a result I can't say, but I hope you find this collection entertaining.

Dominic Garnett, Autumn 2014

Acknowledgements: The author would like to give a huge thanks to: Garrett Fallon, Steve Partner, Paulina Mroczynska, Stuart at the Printing House and all the Garnetts but especially my mother and father. Merlin Unwin, Neville Fickling, Paul Monkman. Simon Jefferies and everyone at Turrall, Stephen Stones, Kevin Wilmot. And a big shout out to all of the following plus a stack of others I have probably forgotten, who keep the spirit of fishing and my enthusiasm in general alive and kicking: Norbert Darby, Geoff Hatt, Russell Hilton, Ian Nadin, Nathan Edgell, Dave Smith, Paul Hamilton, Steve Cullen, Martin Smith, Seb Nowosiad, Simon Blaydes, Jeff Hatt, Dicky Fisk, Jim Smith, Aidan Curran, Adam Aplin, Chris Lambert, Adam Moxey, Alex Prouse, Mike Ferguson, Will Barnard, Chris Tarrant, Bob James, Scott West, Dilip Sarkar. Paul Sharman, John Cheyne, Will Smith and all at the Angling Trust, Dan Sales, Peter Wardle, Pete Gregory, Steve Moore, Julian Chidgey, Eric Edwards and all at the PAC.

Unless stated, all images are copyright of the author. Additional Picture credits, with many thanks: Ian Nadin (p18,19,84,85,87), Paulina Mroczynska (p55), James Callison (p79), John Garnett (81,83), Paul Sharman (p52,53), Frazer McBain and Dave Smith (p23).

A TALE OF TWO HALVES

No angler forgets the day they caught their first pike. My own story involves a dodgy plug and a stroke of good fortune.

Whether it is that strange mixture of fear and wonder, or just their sheer savage beauty, no fish etches itself in the memory in quite the same way as the pike. My first encounters with the toothy one were quite accidental, admittedly. A small roach on the line one moment, bloody history the next, seized in a mass of teeth and flared gills. Genuine heart attack material.

These were not fish to my tender imagination, but monsters from another world, dwarfing and terrorising those little roach and gudgeon that were then my typical catch on the river. As well as fascination, it was fear that captivated me.

Perhaps the tipping point was a family Christmas present of a rather cheap looking jointed plug. Cheap, yes, but it wiggled quite beautifully, at least to a twelve year old boy. A plan was hatched. I knew exactly where a fine pike lived. There was a deep hole underneath the banks of the River Culm, from which she would emerge in the blink of an eye to steal your roach or dace and generally fray nerves. The idea of trying to catch this beast had existed only as a vague concept, until then.

So, on the next trip to the river, a glass fibre spinning rod was set up at the ready for the monster's next appearance. Anything but subtle, she didn't take long to show up that morning, sliding out ominously from beneath the bank and scaring virtually every small fish in the county. With trembling fingers I cast the plug. My garish little present did its sexy, cheap wiggle, like a gaudily dressed hooker prospecting a new street.

A few casts later and I was wondering if that tacky plug was capable of fooling anything,

when WHAM! Perhaps sick of watching this seedy, repetitive dance for the eleventh time the pike surged out and destroyed it in a moment of primeval violence. I nearly died of shock. The pike shook her head from side to side in a fury, like a terrier being electrocuted. The little rod bent obscenely under the strain, before everything went slack.

Total disaster. The jointed plug had given way in the middle and I was left with only the front half and a sick, empty feeling in my belly. Worse still, the pike was now swimming around somewhere with the lure's tail in its jaw, like an unwanted piercing.

About all that I could do was to cast again, this time with an old copper spinner. I tried the same spot. I tried fast and I tried slow. I tried upstream and downstream. It seemed futile. I must have cast that spinner a hundred times, my only incentive the thought of leaving that magnificent pike tethered to half a tasteless plug.

My heart sank when my dad said we would have to leave shortly. I kept recasting, regardless, more in blind hope than expectation, bringing the spinner back past that same undercut lair. Just as my brother was packing up his rod, the line went solid. The pike was back on and as angry as ever! I held on hard as both the spinning rod and my heart started to thump. "Not so hard!" pleaded my father, loosening the drag a little as she flailed in midstream. Her power was amplified by the weight of the current, the reel doing an impression of a coffee grinder as I held on tight and prayed.

After a brutal fight that seemed to last forever but was probably only a few tense minutes, she was in the net. The pike weighed six pounds, an absolute monster to my young eyes. She was the most awesome, perfect fish I had ever seen. We removed the broken half plug first, before taking out the spinner. I watched her swim off with as much relief as joy, hands still trembling. She bolted straight back to her lair underneath the bank, each of us having learned an important lesson about steering well clear of cheap plugs, no matter how sexy their wiggle. ●

IN THE CLEAR

Observing clear water pike at close quarters is always a fascinating experience. On occasion it can force us to reconsider our whole understanding of the species.

The thing didn't move. Not a twitch other than the barely perceptible motion of gills. Not so much a case of slow motion as no motion. For all the world, you might have taken the great fish for a dead, sunken log, an anonymous "it". The pike was just a dark shape, until it registered to view, emerging from the background in a startling moment of clarity, like a picture puzzle that suddenly resolves.

IN THE CLEAR

How on earth did you miss her, this sleeping, metre-long assassin? So peaceful looking, despite the threat. Little fish swam all around her, like a gang of small children playing next to a hulking psychopath. As oblivious as I had been moments earlier, they had no idea that death was just sitting there, watching.

I never cast to that pike. I scarcely knew one end of a wire trace from another at the time. I doubt she would have reacted to much in any case. But I was captivated. The experience is one that has stayed with me, forming a vivid impression many years on, a spell that I still haven't escaped from.

Perhaps the biggest draw of pike fishing for me is its strong visual aspect. Observing pike is almost a pursuit in itself, something magical, absorbing, sometimes startling. I have spent many hours drawn to small, clear waters purely because I love the game of hide and seek they represent.

No matter what you know, or think you know, pike always have that capacity to surprise and I remain convinced that they are not the stupid, fearless creatures of angling cliches. All of the observations that follow are first hand. Attempting to decipher or explain every detail is no way to preserve the fun and mystery of the exercise however, so I invite the reader to draw their own conclusions.

FOOD FIGHT

It is a cold, clear day in January on a skinny little canal. The section I'm exploring is as shallow as a boy band. There are many different degrees of visibility you might encounter on any given visit, from pea soup to aquarium clear. Today is off the scale, the sort of occasion you can see the bottom even in the depths of the dead centre, where you can pick out each dead leaf and empty bottle on the deck as if it were trapped in glass. But where are the pike?

It is a hypnotic challenge, stalking this little channel. A game best played with patience and a decent pair of polarising glasses, or "x-ray specs" as I like to call them.

Be warned: if you gaze into the canal for long enough, the canal gazes back. For every few yards that are deserted save the odd stick or rogue perch, a little further on is a pike, lying still but ever watchful. Sometimes when you stop and take a closer look these lone fish multiply into a gang before your very eyes.

My first target is easily spotted, a jack of perhaps no more than three pounds, gently moving along the far bank. One false move can blow the whole plan and so, stooping down, I ease into position, hook a sprat and guide it carefully towards the fish. The bait lands gently, a few feet away. The jack reacts almost instantly, turning towards the splash. There is no hurry, no fearless smash and grab. Slowly but surely it closes the gap on the bait, a silver-white flank I can pick out clearly against the dark silt of the bottom. It is at this moment I spot a second, slightly bigger pike also in close proximity. To my surprise, this one also homes in on the bait. Just as the smaller fish thinks about making a grab, the larger pike rushes towards the smaller rival, bullying him away in a short but vigorous, nose to tail chase.

The second pike is still in no hurry having seen off the first and turns slowly towards the bait, hovering for a few moments before

Tangles with Pike 11

edging closer once again. But he's too slow: a third pike, bigger again, has the same idea and pushes forward with intent to see what the commotion is about. I can't believe I didn't spot this fish, the biggest of the trio, which has undoubtedly had a cold eye on the whole scene all along. This time there is no need for confrontation—pike number two sulks off as if accepting its place in the snapping order yet too proud to fly away in panic.

For the so-called "freshwater shark" each fish has shown a notable degree of poise. None of the three has been in a rush. Pike approaching dead baits in clear, cold water seldom are. The whole drama takes a few minutes to unfold, before finally the victor sidles up to the sprat until it is an inch or two in front of its nose. Pointed jaws billow open and the little silver flank of bait disappears.

The pike feels the pressure as I strike and goes kiting off along the cut, silt clouding up in its wake. She's a beautifully wild and lean looking creature, no more than seven pounds but already seeing off smaller rivals. I release

"Be warned: if you gaze into the canal for long enough, the canal gazes back."

the fish quickly and carefully, shaking my head at what I've just seen and pondering if a fourth pike in the chain lies waiting nearby.

CORNERED

On some clear water days, every pike in a stretch seems to be sleeping. On other, rarer occasions the reverse can be true. The game of hide and seek on a small drain then becomes far simpler as the roach shoals get nervous and pike reveal themselves in motion. Sometimes it is just as you are walking back to the car before evening that a seemingly empty stretch of water suddenly comes alive as pike of all sizes creep out from their hiding places to spy a closer look at dinner.

Perhaps the holy grail of sightings for any pike watcher is to witness an actual hunt in progress. I am talking about natural behaviour, of course, and not the capture of any bait we have presented, thrilling though this can also be. The sudden heave of water and sight of silver fish flipping clear of the water in panic is a spectacle in itself you might see many times. If you're really lucky you may even witness the kill itself. On one occasion I watched an attacker tail my pike fly before seizing a small roach instead. On another I remember seeing a jack grab a fish that looked slightly too big for it crossways, like a dog with a bone. This wrestling match lasted several minutes before the prey fish was successfully turned and swallowed.

Another sighting that stands out for me occurred on a clear drain as I stared into the margin on a perfectly overcast autumn day. Small fish had been scattering and I witnessed roach fleeing for the bank side, no longer in the safety of numbers but what appeared to be the nervous fragments of a shoal. Is this how pike sometimes pick off prey, by scattering the group? Crouching absolutely still, I saw a pike of eight, perhaps ten pounds follow a fair sized roach right into the margin. A curious stalemate ensued. The roach swam tight into the bank, while the pursuer followed before stopping some two feet away, alert and poised to strike. For what seemed like an eternity but was probably just a few tense seconds, neither adversary dared to make a move.

Sometimes you can tell when a pike is about to rush forward, as its fins and tail give a slight tremble, almost like a cat gives a little wiggle to align itself before pouncing. A split second rush of attack was followed by rocking water, swaying reeds and the pike making off along the bank. Whether this was a kill or a near miss I can only speculate.

A CAUTIONARY TALE

Most anglers will be familiar with the phenomenon of pike that follow but don't bite, but just how much of a part does caution play? It is a myth that predators are mindless killers; in truth most born hunters display a wide range of behaviour, from sudden aggression to stealthy cunning.

It is a spring morning on the deep, reed-strewn banks of Exeter Canal. The waters are clear and weedy. I can see the silver shine of my wobbled roach several feet down as I let it flutter and pause in the still water. It must be cast fifty-something before a long shape comes snaking after the bait. The pike hangs in the water, just shy of the bank. I crouch absolutely still and let the bait drop and lie still. The pike swims away.

IN THE CLEAR

Two casts later and the sequence is repeated, the fish hanging in the water just in front of me cautiously, fins rippling. I give a twitch; no response. The bait settles on the bottom and I pause. This time the pike, which looks around six pounds, slowly angles itself downwards and comes closer to my offering. We both freeze, neither able to make our minds up. After another few tense moments, impatience get the better of me and I try another twitch. Unimpressed, the pike gently swims away again, just out of sight.

On the third attempt, I throw the bait just a little further out, leaving it static again and this time vowing not to move until the roach disappears. What follows is startling. Sure enough, my quarry returns. Again, the roach is studied for a few long moments. The pike then edges right up to the bait and gives what I can only describe as a suspicious little prod with its snout. Can it see wire and hooks? Has it seen me? I can only guess. The fish swims away again. This time it doesn't return.

PIT FIGHT

A windswept gravel pit is not always the best place to observe pike, in spite of the usually clear water. It is easy enough to imagine the pike to be out in the beyond, somewhere outside our field of vision. A simple mistake to make.

Picture a bitterly cold afternoon on a pit of epic proportions. Dead baits thrown well out into the deeps pass the day unmolested. The sailed vane of a large drifter float works beautifully in the wind but refuses to dip. I wade to the edge of a reed line at intervals to have another throw. The water around my legs, no more than two and a half feet deep, looks tempting. But surely too shallow for pike? Besides, my size fourteens have probably put out enough of a warning signal.

"I strike instantly and she goes ballistic, putting several yards between us in the blink of an eye."

The moment of truth comes as I prepare for another long throw. My still frozen bait has an awkward buoyancy and so I test it beside the reeds, trying to ensure it sits right, just off the deck. I'm still idly checking the bait when I catch something out of the corner of my eye and do an almighty double take. Some three feet from my boots, a long, dark shape emerges.

Am I hallucinating? A decent pike in only inches of near freezing water? I lift the bait again and this seals it; without hesitation the fish makes a grab. I strike instantly and she goes ballistic, putting several yards between us in the blink of an eye. The rod arcs round and the reeds heave. I wade towards the commotion and the pike bursts away again, thrashing in the shallow water.

At a scrape under ten pounds, this close encounter has been a very welcome surprise. Having retreated to the shelter of the car, my brother misses the day's only five minutes of drama. Nothing but biting cold follows.

FAIR OR FOUL?

We end our handful of encounters almost where we started, with another case of the slumbering giant. On this occasion it was my father who spotted "sleeping beauty", a good-sized fish that remained absolutely stock still. You may well have experienced the same phenomenon too. Cast after cast with no response, it can be a bit like trying to pick a fight with a stiff. In the case of a small jack you just keep walking, but when it is a big fish playing hard to get, you keep trying. And trying.

On this occasion we were using fly rods. Having had several jacks on little fry imitations, a fingerling roach pattern went on first. No reply. Next came a bigger fly, surely a better option for a bigger pike? No reply. How about a brighter fly? Same again. Fast, slow, skimming the surface and scraping the bottom; nothing worked. The fish remained like a statue throughout while half my father's box of flies was paraded past its nose. I am reminded of those Royal guards who don't flinch even when you pull ridiculous faces at them. Nevertheless, my dad kept trying whilst I scratched my head. You could have held a rock festival right there on the bank without any reaction.

Eventually something worked, although it is with trepidation that I continue here. My father, whose eyesight is admittedly not eagle-sharp, landed a cast tight across the pike's nose. As the fly reached close to those jaws, he gave a twitch. I would love to tell you that at this point the pike sucked in the fly. What actually happened was that the pike still didn't budge an inch; the fly simply stuck in its chin. Incredibly, it still gave no reaction. We watched it for a few brief seconds, sitting there with the fly sticking out of its chin like a strange, coloured beard. Dad pulled ever so gently; the pike stayed dead still. Another little pluck and she gave a tremor. Only with a firmer pull did the fish finally react in full-blooded fashion, hurtling off at speed. Fly line shot out after the beast, the reel fairly buzzing to let out extra line in response.

After a short but violent fight we had her on the mat, a beautiful twelve pounder. I removed the barbless fly from her chin somewhat sheepishly for a quick return. The only thing I can say in my old man's defence is that the whole sorry means of capture was quite accidental. ●

LOST IN SOMERSET

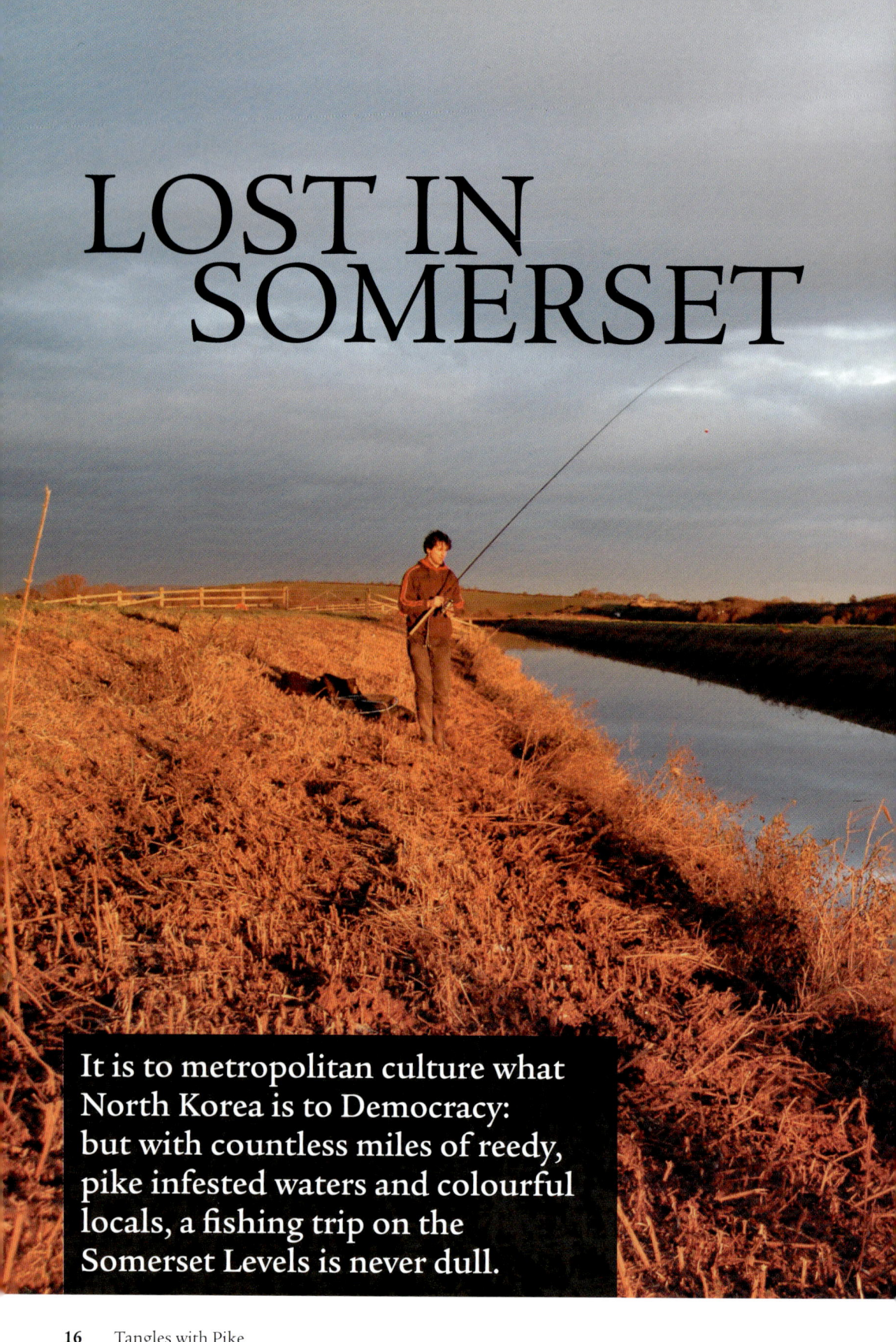

It is to metropolitan culture what North Korea is to Democracy: but with countless miles of reedy, pike infested waters and colourful locals, a fishing trip on the Somerset Levels is never dull.

"A historic part of the Westcountry" say the brochures. "Friendly market towns, local fare and regional history". The truth is that I don't visit Somerset in search of culture—I come here to escape from it. I come here in search of a great back of beyond, a wild criss-crossed tangle of slow, weedy rivers and endless manmade channels where the pike are fierce and the maps get vague. The Somerset Levels. A place that may as well be a million miles away from the republic of traffic jams and Tescos. Bleak, flat, and muddy. Toothy monsters and chewed up land.

Somerset, bloody Somerset. Just getting there in one piece is an adventure in itself. Today is no exception, from villages with whitewashed signs to the rusted fences and muddy, unmarked tracks the PR people must have missed. But eventually all the wrong

LOST IN SOMERSET

"Whoever called this place of dropping slopes the 'Levels' clearly never tried to find a flat place to park their backside."

turns and bad directions end and the river stretches out before me, oddly straight and unfaltering. Mile after mile of steep banks and solitude, just cattle for company. Stark and unforgiving. Bloody beautiful.

A look at the water soon dampens the soul and removes any romantic illusions however. The river is murky, high and dull, a scenario that sums up the gulf between my midweek daydreams and the altogether more sobering reality of a boggy Sunday morning in January. Clear water and a day's fly fishing are hastily replaced by a bag of dead herrings to be lobbed into this muddy soup; art gives way to business.

Still, watching the yellow top of a juicy pike float is not the worst thing in the world. It's even better when you actually get bites. But with nothing stirring I keep moving and watching, searching and waiting, wishing I had more layers on, wishing I had prepared a hot flask of tea rather than extra pike flies.

The steep sides of the bank are rough and bare. Whoever called this place of dropping slopes the "Levels" clearly never tried to find a flat place to park their backside. The whole landscape has been transformed into a wasteland in the floods and the cold.

The float bobs constantly, not with the attention of hungry pike but the constant tow of swollen water, assorted debris fouling the line. I survey the tide's latest deposits: Today's free gifts include plastic bags, cider cans and a broken doll, stained features gazing inanely at the sky. Previous highlights include women's shoes, a single hotdog sausage in a jar and a copy of "Beverley Hills Cop 2" spewing black ribbons from an ancient VHS tape, which I dared a friend to return to the rentals section at the local post office.

Teeth gritted, I scan further upstream, looking for a clue in this featureless straight, the wind whistling in the scrub. So far all that exists is hope and muddy water. A very different reality from the clear depths I plundered here not so long back.

A perverse pleasure, this winter pike fishing. Adversity? We pike anglers damned well invented it. Like a gruelling run or starving yourself before a hearty meal there is, admittedly, a pleasure in the punishment, something satisfying about striving against the odds. Up to a point, you understand. If I was in the marketing business I would call this a "character building" experience. In plain English I am sodding cold and rapidly losing enthusiasm. The pike are usually modest but plentiful here but do not like high, coloured water any more than the angler. For better or worse, I must follow my instincts and move.

More rutted tracks and unmarked roads follow. More dark clouds. A face off with a rusty Land rover and its mad driver, all threadbare jumper and murderer's eyes. Basic manners, let alone indicating where you're going, are unheard of out here. But this is not my back yard and it's none of my business where anyone is going. More miles clock up,

Tangles with Pike **19**

the roads seeming to bear little resemblance to the map I'm looking at.

Plan B is a secluded little drain. A little improvement, perhaps? More chocolate coloured water greets me, this time along with a random local and his vanload of dead and dying plant material. Poking out of his worn sleeves are two of the filthiest human hands I have ever seen. "The outdoors type", to put it politely. In other words he looks like he just emerged from a ditch. But there is a sparkle in his eye as I mention pike fishing and his eyebrows raise into life. A grubby finger points into the waterlogged beyond, where the pike are so big that only the foulest possible language could ever do them justice.

Galvanized by such fantasies, I trudge on down the bank, my numb limbs straining to carry too much gear in too much of a hurry. The wind picks up again and attacks face and fingers. Drizzle dampened, I keep walking and scanning the dank water.

Half hour shifts come and go in each spot. Each move brings fresh hope, before giving way to restlessness and an uneasy feeling of impotence against this land of battered reeds and green flood water. At least when I used to smoke I could keep a little something busy, a little industry during the lulls. I consider idly the thought of going home and returning on some more favourable day; a pretty laughable idea when you're lost on a boggy drain, fifty miles from home.

My trousers are wet and so are my feet. Is it any wonder that so little romantic prose exists

> "A grubby finger points into the waterlogged beyond, where the the pike are so big that only the foulest possible language could ever do them justice."

about winter pike angling? This is sport for real men, tough souls with thick jumpers and stout hearts. This is no gentlemanly pursuit but a form of masochism. Sure, anyone can catch a pike when the air is mild and the water clear and inviting. They seem to be everywhere on those temperate days of autumn. Three months on and the fish have been entirely obscured, painted over.

It's all a confidence trick, I keep telling myself. Somewhere down in the soup before me is the pike I'm after, I keep telling myself. She might not like high, cold water any more than I do, but if I can just pitch my herring close enough to her nose then there is a chance. Somewhere, a chance. Just a matter of providing temptation in the right place, like dropping a bag of chips next to a sleeping drunk.

At last, there is a knock on the float tip. The gentle "dink, dink" of interest. Another shudder and the float starts to submerge, creeping off almost casually. In my mind's eye I can see a great metre long fish, numberless teeth, gills pushing wide as she inhales the bait and gently moves off. An unceremonious strike and we are connected. A few seconds thrashing later and a very different pike comes tamely to the net. Not the fish of a lifetime but a pale, angry looking jack of two or three pounds, more teeth than belly, more fight on the bank than in the water.

It's a start, I tell myself. But moments later the tow of green water becomes amplified to ridiculous proportions, accelerated suddenly by unseen forces, very probably an opening floodgate. You never quite know what the Levels will be like on the day since the dozens of rivers, channels, ditches and drains are all connected by intersections, gates and pumping stations, the mechanics of which are quite beyond me.

The fishing turns from unappealing to downright foolhardy. By this time options are running out. The sun has made its first cameo appearance but it scarcely seems to matter by now. Without a second thought I just move on. With numb fingers I bundle rods, muddy kit and crossed lines into the boot and drive. I flush out all thoughts of fire places and strong drink. I turn down a lane some eight miles away, ignoring a bent and whitewashed sign, off to the canal this time. It is more curiosity than genuine hope that pulls at me by this stage. Just one more spot, I tell myself.

A moment of surprised delirium follows. Clear water. Not bottle-and-drink-it clear, but clear enough for renewed hope. In one or two places I can even spot that old friend of mine, the bottom. A pack of little perch swing past gingerly. Signs of life are here and my cue is duly taken. Sod the herrings, out comes the fly rod.

Drizzle slowly gives way to sunshine as I make my way along the towpath with a lighter step. How quickly things can turn. A big, glittery creation fits the bill perfectly and soon the smooth, brightly coloured fly line arcs across the canal. This expanse of rotting lily stems and gloomy corners is no Monet painting but simply oozes weedy promise. I can feel that buzz of excitement return to my fingers as I work a lively retrieve. The big tease soon pays off. A bulge by the reeds and the rod explodes to life. My second spindly jack of the day comes in. This one is a beautifully

> "The rod kicks bullishly, building to a deep, dangerous curve. Scrambling down the bank a few yards I blaze slack line back on the reel, feeling her bump and thrash somewhere in the depths of the canal's central track."

marked riot of teeth and spots. No matter, I rediscover my sense of humour in the warmth of the afternoon sun.

For the next two hours it's carnival time, a glorious afternoon which is all the more delirious because it is totally unexpected. After several hours drizzle and muddy disappointment comes a zen-like spell of fishing. The next pike results from a fishing moment as pure as any chalk stream sycophant raves about. About two-thirds across the canal little silver blades fly out of the water, fleeing in panic. Their pursuer slams across the surface sending wide shock waves bulging. A hasty cast lands some five feet beyond this murder scene. Three or four jerks and the fly line slams tight. A brief but satisfyingly berserk fight follows as a better pike attempts to destroy my fly rod. Even beside the bank, this one doesn't think the argument is over and I'm grateful to slip out the barbless hook and let him fly off to look for a healthier snack.

The onslaught continues from here, pike attacking from the far bank, near bank and even the centre of the canal, slashing at the fly from reedy straights, emerging from shady corners to pounce. After several fish of the small but psychotic variety smash the fly the next take, from the depths of the middle, is a sneakier affair. It starts with the gentlest little shudder. I stop momentarily and notice the fly line snaking off to one side. A firm lift and there is a solid weight on the other end.

The line continues in its course along the canal, along and away. It is only when I pull harder that the fish wakes up, accelerating away. The rod kicks bullishly, building to a deep, dangerous curve. Scrambling down the bank a few yards I blaze slack line back on the reel, feeling her bump and thrash somewhere in the depths of the canal's central track. As I catch up she flies for the far bank and I apply the brakes. She turns inches from the reeds, a solid, golden-green flank, heaving against the pressure. The pike comes in stubbornly, a foot or two at a time, until I can slide the net under her and the last thrash of water is merely one last protest. She is lean and muscular, faultlessly spotted; ten pounds, perhaps even a little bigger. It seems pretty irrelevant and in any case the scales are with the bag of dead herrings and the kitchen sink in the car. I take just a few seconds to marvel at her, holding the fish upright in the cold water before she kicks out of my grasp, sailing out of reach once again.

Moments later this perfect and unexpected spell of drama comes to an abrupt close. A motorized barge ploughs through the water straight past my position, turning the water into chocolate milkshake; hopeless for fly fishing.

"Any good?" shouts the man on the deck. I just smile and make that universal, half-arsed "so-so" signal with my free hand. My feet are heavy with clay as I trudge back tired but satisfied, the fine little teeth cuts in my fingers testament to a good days fishing in spite of everything. Some days you win, some you lose. Sometimes you feel privileged to just have survived while catching a few fish. ●

REINVENTING A LOST ART

It's a versatile, ultra natural and deadly effective method. It catches big fish where both dead baits and lures fail. So why is wobbling for pike such a forgotten art form?

Clumsy, out-dated rigs, general misunderstanding and catalogues full of flashy lures seem to have relegated the art of wobbling to dusty books, rusted hooks and Victorian gentleman with daft surnames. Indeed how many of us have bothered to try, let alone persevere with the method?

Of course, you'll never know until you give it a try, but wobbling offers distinct advantages. Firstly, it provides a completely natural presentation that can fool the wisest predator, even on a water that has been bombarded with all manner of lures. A wobbled natural bait can also be worked tantalizingly at any depth, ultra slowly if necessary. This is especially useful in cold conditions and for those big, wily specimens that are rarely inclined to chase gaudy, fast moving pieces of plastic or metal.

There is simply nothing for a pike to fear in a bait such as a roach—it looks right, gives off an attractive scent and can even be left completely static for a following predator to pick up at leisure. In contrast to lure or fly fishing, you'll find very few times when a follower refuses to have a chomp.

The penny really dropped for me when I beat my previous bests on waters I had, prior to this, fished only with lures or static dead baits. But it took some tinkering. It is a simple fact that many anglers are put off wobbling

A new rig that led to the capture of my first twenty-pound pike was the subject of this Pike and Predators article on wobbling or "sink and draw" tactics. As the first piece of writing on fishing I ever had published, it brings back a certain nostalgia, along with a tinge of sadness that James Holgate, the editor at the time who gave me that first all important break, is no longer with us. This story remains true to the original text, although the rig shown is an improved version.

REINVENTING A LOST ART

because the crude rigs used are just a recipe for frustration. The average, textbook wobbling rig is basically just a dead bait trace with the fish hooked the other way round. Bait losses are high and the action tends to be stiff and unnatural. Most who try run out of patience (or bait!) pretty quickly

The breakthrough came from sabotaging a few items of carp tackle. By using a large bait clip to attach the dead bait through both lips I found big advantages. The offering could be locked in place with great security, to the extent that the bait stayed put even when a pike had torn half the body off. Better still, attached in this way, the bait had far better freedom of movement and could wobble in any direction.

The results spoke for themselves. The pike went ballistic for an altogether more seductive wobble, while I lost far fewer baits than before. In the months that followed my lures started to gather dust.

TACKLE BREAKDOWN

Tackle itself needn't be overcomplicated and the emphasis should be on simplicity and mobility. Typical lure fishing tackle will suit most of your wobbling needs. It goes without saying that you must have a large net, unhooking tools and a suitable mat. Pike conservation should be a top priority for all of us.

As for rod choice, I am not a fan of either spindly little lure rods or beefy jerk bait rods. A reliable, balanced spinning rod with power in the butt and a sensitive tip to impart life into the bait is ideal. A nine or ten foot model is the ideal length, giving much better reach and control over a fish where bankside snags exist. Couple this with a reliable fixed spool or multiplier reel. For the sake of safety as well as performance I prefer to use braided line of thirty pounds or greater strength. When you hook that monster that ploughs through

Rig components

1

2

26   Tangles with Pike

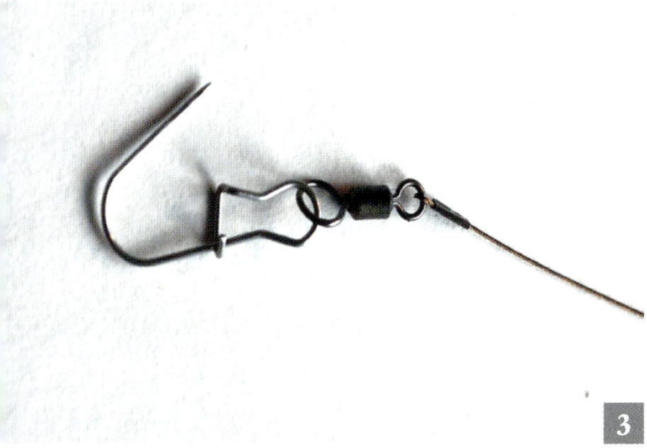

RIG CONSTRUCTION

Components: The materials you'll need are as pictured below: Tough wire, pliers, size 4 treble hook, swivel/ specialist swivel, bait flag, a large snap link, plus a hook sharpener or small file.

Step 1: Begin by taking pliers, opening up your snap link and bending the locking arm straight (not all snaps work—this is a Kaliber snap link)

Step 2: Once the locking arm is as straight as you can get it, use a file or hook sharpener to work it to a sharp, fine point.

Step 3: Attach the new clip to the larger eye of a specialist swivel as shown (a large conventional swivel will also work). Just out of the picture here, we have 18" of strong wire, attached to another swivel.

Step 4: Now tie or crimp a size four treble hook to a short length of wire and fasten to the eye of the swivel, as shown. Length can vary according to your typical bait size. Big baits can take rigs with two trebles.

Step 5: A correctly mounted bait. The only other adjustment you might make is to add a squeeze of lead putty or a shot just above the swivel to increase the sink rate, or an internal wobbling bar (I cut my own from lengths of mild steel and whip to a length of wire to anchor to the rig).

Tangles with Pike 27

> "Avoid cheap tackle at all costs and opt for tough, high quality hooks, snap links and swivels. Remember that a big pike will quickly find any weakness in your kit."

half a ton of weed you will understand my reasoning! Braid also offers superb bite detection and allows complete control of the bait, even at distance.

Finally, at the business end, avoid cheap tackle at all costs and opt for tough, high quality hooks, snap links and swivels. Remember that a big pike will quickly find any weakness in your kit.

WOBBLING BAITS

The list of baits that can be used for wobbling is long: roach, perch, sprats, trout, smelt and scores of others all work. However, my number one choice is the humble roach, since they are not only durable but form the staple diet of pike on so many waters and are totally natural so as to be taken by the wiliest of pike. Optimum size is a bait of four to six inches in my opinion, which will cast well and be easily engulfed by almost any pike that swims.

Bigger baits may be worth experimenting with, but they come off more easily, require heavier tackle and seem clumsy by comparison. Contrary to popular myth, pike can also be easily spooked by big, splashy baits, especially in shallow water.

A supply of bait for several sessions can be harvested with light tackle. Please remember to take baits from the water you intend to fish. Dispatch them humanely (I use a trout priest) and take them only from areas where they are abundant. Of course, if this is too much hassle, blast frozen roach are almost as good.

If roach are unavailable, then smelts, sprats or scad are all useful baits. Sprats are especially good value and make a good back up when the roach run out (and for the record I do also like these and other baits dyed when visibility is poor).

A wobbled bait can be fished in exactly the same areas you might work a lure. Being a visible method it requires some degree of water clarity for best results, although the smell of the bait will help in murkier conditions. Cover of all kinds such as reeds, bushes, weed beds and structures are ideal, as are areas rich in prey fish, underwater features and changes of depth (you probably know the drill by now). Having fished extensively on rivers and even more on canals, the "shelf" where shallow and deeper water meet is an absolutely key area.

Unlike with standard lures, you can work these areas as slowly and tantalizingly as you dare. You can jerk the bait high in the water over sunken weed, for example, or you can let it sink right to the bottom and trip it along at a snail's pace, brilliant for tough winter conditions. You can even make the bait stop dead for a few moments, which is ideal for sluggish predators or when a reluctant fish follows but needs time to make its mind up. I have taken plenty of pike by leaving the bait static in this fashion, which is thrilling stuff in clear water.

Traditionally the "wobbling" action was created by putting a bend in the bait. You can try this to get a provocative, exaggerated movement, but I find a stiff, corkscrewing action poor and unnatural looking, to my eyes at least. With the improved rig it is also unnecessary.

Rather than fasten my hook in the flank of the bait under tension, I prefer to leave

Early tinkering with rigs led to the capture of this fine canal fish, my first ever twenty-pounder.:

just a touch of slack, to let the bait wobble completely freely from the head. I also like the treble to pull out of the bait and into the jaw of the pike easily on the strike.

Getting a really deadly action with a wobbled bait is not rocket science, but takes just a little practice and dexterity. You must think about what you are trying to achieve: the impression of a dying, sickly or panicking prey fish. Time spent observing sick or distressed fish will give you the right idea and I like my wobbled bait to look so diseased and cranky that biting its head off would be doing it a favour! In fact the old term "sink and draw" is instructive in suggesting a fluttering, stop-start motion.

Remember that this is not lure fishing. You do not need to constantly move your bait to convince your quarry that it is alive; you are using a real fish! Having said that, a dead roach has no in-built action. However, you will find that even the slightest twitch of the rod tip of flick of the reel handle will give terrific gliding, darting and dying motions. Be imaginative, experimental and above all don't feel the need to rush. Far too many anglers crank their baits or lures in at such speed they never explore at depth or give those bigger, lazier pike time to strike. In deeper water don't be afraid to count your bait right down and work it back gently.

> "The beauty of wobbling is its sheer versatility. If the pike are in a chasing mood you can employ a quicker, snappier retrieve. If they are lethargic and holding deeper, you can creep the bait along as slowly as you wish."

THE TAKE

Detecting and hitting takes when wobbling requires a different approach to lure fishing. Surprisingly few bites will be violent, smash-and-grab affairs and indeed, much of the time all you will feel is a pluck or tightening of the line. Sometimes the bite will feel like weed or the bottom, until you suddenly feel something shifting.

At any indication you should react by dropping the rod tip for an instant to give a little slack, before lifting firmly. There is no need to delay the strike by any more than a brief pause however, since it is usually patently obvious what is happening. The most I will wait is a count to three before striking and I find most of my fish really easy to unhook, meaning less need for excessive handling and time out of the water, which is beneficial to both pike and angler. (You'll also notice that my standard rig has only one treble hook too—much kinder to the pike). The odd fish you lose will tend to be the tiny jack that couldn't manage to engulf the bait fully in the first place.

It is also worth remembering to strike quite hard. A half-hearted strike is probably the most common cause of losing fish early in the fight. Quite often the pike will purely be holding onto the bait and with a weak strike the fish is not actually hooked but simply unwilling to let go until you pull back harder and it's a case of "see you later."

VARIATIONS

The beauty of wobbling is its sheer versatility. If the pike are in a chasing mood you can employ a quicker, snappier retrieve. If they are lethargic and holding deeper, you can creep the bait along as slowly as you wish. The method can be used in conjunction with, or directly compared to, dead baits or lures on the day too. Indeed, the more you explore and experiment, the more success you will enjoy with this deadly, underused method.

One favourite trick I learned from pike anglers in Ireland is a particular way to combine wobbling and dead baiting. Using two rods, one set up for each method, a static bait is cast out while another wobbled offering is used to search the surrounding water each time bringing the wobbled bait past the static dead. Sometimes the pike will respond best to the moving bait, while other days the wobbled fish is not taken as often but will lead the pike to the dead bait, which represents an even easier meal and is promptly devoured. This can give the best of both methods and encourages the angler to stay alert and mobile.

Lure fishermen too, can benefit from wobbling. In fact, you could easily tie some versions of the rig shown with just the final swivel and business end attachments, allowing you to slip it onto a lure fisherman's snap link in seconds. All lure anglers are familiar with the problem of pike that follow but refuse to take. Wobbling can catch these fish and we can even deliberately set out to use lures as an attractor before picking off reluctant predators with real bait. I like to use out and out attractors like spinnerbaits or vigorous rattling lures to wake up the pike

This bucket-mouthed fish of 23lbs 10oz took a wobbled skimmer.

and bring them out. If they won't take, I have a handful of baits and rigs with me to quickly switch over.

Naturally, if you fish clear waters wobbling set ups can also be used to simply free-line baits to pike. If you cast to a fish that is sleepy or just browses without making its mind up, try adding a twitch or two. This often prompts the pike to make its mind up before lunch swims away.

If you are already a "wobbler" I hope my ideas have given you food for thought. For those yet to try it, all I can say is you won't know what you're missing until you give it a go. Take a good supply of bait, tie some rigs in advance and give it a serious trial, not half an hour when the going is slow. If your local venue is hard fished with standard tactics it could be a revelation. However, it will work on all kinds of waters and in my experience seems to catch a disproportionate number of bigger than average pike. Crap rigs are no longer an excuse, so what are you waiting for? Go forth and wobble! ●

THE MONSTER AND THE JERK

There are days in pike fishing where the highlight is the hot bath when you get home. But there are also those days that will stay with you forever. Such was my trip to a midlands reservoir with lure maker Alex Prouse.

Looking across wide, choppy waters on a dour autumn day you do sometimes wonder what you're up against. The question "where do I start?" could also apply to the box in front of me today, as lure-maker Alex Prouse lifts the lid. His pride and joy is a rogue's gallery of lovingly made soft plastic jerkbaits. There are lures that look like trout and others like jack pike—paddle shaped tails and long, flowing appendages. An assortment of painted eyes stare up, each of these creatures saying the same thing: "pick me!"

Whichever mutations you favour best, jerkbaits are a real confidence booster where large waters are concerned. They are large, loud and lurid. Even when faced with big empty spaces, these are lures the pike just can't fail to notice. As our first casts touch down with a hearty splash, my first surprise is just how vigorously Alex retrieves his lures.

"It's surprising how high in the water pike will hold up and attack in the autumn," he reveals. "I'll slow down if necessary, but if the pike are active they do like things lively and I've had some of my best days cranking lures back hard."

For over ten years, Alex has been making and field-testing his own brand of large, soft plastic creations. You can see the rewards of his TLC as they return to the boat. The tails move beautifully, bulky bodies roll and turn with each crank.

A far cry from off-the-peg, commercially made models, the thing that strikes you most is the individuality of each lure. It's very much a knack of trying out each artificial and seeing which speed and style of retrieve works best. "I like to throw in at least one 'break' or pause every time I bring the lure back," says Alex. "By making a sudden stop and then speeding up again, you'll often prompt a following fish to take."

The only thing more fun than bringing these beasts to life is the feel of a bone crunching hit from a big pike. The first signs of life occur as I

"I like to throw in at least one 'break' or pause every time I bring the lure back," says Alex. "By making a sudden stop and then speeding up again, you'll often prompt a following fish to take."

witness a good fish in pursuit, which hovers just by the boat. Minutes later, Alex connects with a full-blooded hit. After some head banging in the depths, a double figure pike lashes at the surface. With the hooks visible, Alex decides to chin the fish rather than risk them tangling in the net. He believes in playing pike hard to avoid exhausting them—and after a quick snap or two, she's safely released.

If the lures themselves are full of character, the names are a reflection of this too. The Wagtail, his best selling lure so far, needs little explanation, but what about the infamous "Wobbly Bob" or "Gangster"?

"I was once picking my daughter up from school when I noticed another parent's vehicle had written on it: 'Wobbly Bob's Party Balloons'. The guy had a daft sense of humour and did kids' birthdays. He had a club foot and hence a wobbly walk. I guess the name just stuck!". As for the Gangster, the name arrived after an unexpected phone call. "An American bloke called me out of the blue one day to ask if the name 'Zoota Lures' had any connection with the Zoota family," explains Alex. "The guy was tracing family history and it turns out that the name has an old Mafia connection. One of Al Capone's gang was a Zoota—hence I just had to name one of my lures the Gangster."

Beyond the quirky names and big pike stories however, Alex's tale is one of those great examples of how a "roll your own" attitude to tackle making has led to a rather special success story. "It was quite an outlay at first" he recalls, "but I really got the lure-making bug, and I reasoned that if they didn't sell I'd at least have a lifetime supply of lures."

We cover plenty of acres on today's trip, making various drifts to cover the fish. The pike hit well out from the bank, in anything up to 25ft of water on this occasion. The lures certainly attract a good stamp of pike, one of which makes my jaw drop as it hangs for a second close to the boat. Alex's suggestion for those infuriating fish which follow but won't bite is to drop down a size or two, in this case to a Mini Wagtail—still a good mouthful but a little easier to grab whole.

Just ten minutes later and the line draws solid as the bite-sized jerkbait is seized. Slow, thumping pressure immediately tells me this is no jack. A steady pull brings the fish to the surface. What I witness next makes me slightly weak at the knees. Not only am I attached to perhaps the longest pike I have ever hooked,

Tangles with Pike 35

> "What I witness next makes me slightly weak at the knees. Not only am I attached to perhaps the longest pike I have ever hooked, but we are connected only by the merest nick of the rear treble."

but we are connected only by the merest nick of the rear treble.

I increase the pressure as much as I dare and the fish starts to wallow. By this stage I'm praying she doesn't decide to come up and shake her head. Meanwhile, Alex is busy taking a couple of snaps. "Sod the camera—just grab the net!" are my desperate words. The pressure builds again, but I manage to turn her. Second by agonizing second, she nears the boat. The net heaves, the fish gives a thrash and the lure, which doesn't look so big any more, comes free in an instant.

more than I did, but he won't have any of this. "I've had just as big a kick over the last few years seeing what the lures have caught other anglers. It was worth it just to see the look on your face!" he laughs at me.

It's not the first big pike to be taken on one of his unique jerkbaits by any stretch, nor will it be the last, as Alex proves with a formidable twenty-pound pike of his own just a couple of drifts later.

So, what will you decide to throw at the pike next time you get a day on Chew, Loch Lomond or Grafham? A mass-produced plug the pike have seen a dozen times? My next cast will be with one of Alex's handmade specials. I might even start with the lure that tempted my monster, if he'll sell it to me. "That lure just got a lot more expensive," he grins. ●

Twenty-seven pounds and ten ounces seem a wholly inadequate way to express three or so minutes of the most potent tension, awe, joy and sheer relief. After a quick picture and a safe return I still can't quite believe what has happened. If anything, Alex deserved the fish

Sadly, Alex no longer sells his "Zoota Lures", which might be why I've hardly dared make another cast with the magic jerkbait that caught my big pike. I might actually be buried with it.

OF ICE AND MEN

Pike fishing is not a pastime for the faint-hearted. You often have to take on the cold and the vagaries of the seasons as well as the fish. It is a peculiar thrill to catch a pike through a small gap in a stretch of water that is otherwise solid with ice.

Tiverton, sleepy Tiverton. Deadbeat Devon town of bargain stores and the smoky grey shadow of forgotten industry. Bus station, police station, Tescos and tarmac. And yet pretty beneath it all, in places at least, like a fine ornament covered in dust. Curves on a painted bridge, a decrepit cafe and the pale front of an old, frozen looking cinema.

As we cut through the town on a Sunday morning only a sparse few natives are stirring, like spare parts from Saturday night's piss-up still looking for somewhere open. A warren of dusty stores and boozers left somewhere circa 1978. At the end of these second hand streets we find the high school, sprayed names on a cracked bus shelter and yet bright new buildings behind like an experimental collision of crime and progress.

Canal Hill on the outskirts and everything changes. Just a stone's throw from the teen smokers and single mums looms the stately Blundell's School. A place where parents own luxury cars and horses, and where Miles and Freddie are infected with Latin. A strange, almighty mix up, this old Tiverton town.

Our next and final stop before the countryside returns is the last waypoint before the wild frontier of "out of town". By which I mean that one terminal, overpriced but strategically placed garage that always finds you when you're hungry. The place that is always open when

Tangles with Pike   39

OF ICE AND MEN

"Enclosed under this frozen top sheet is another separate and trapped world... The frosts lend a certain beauty to the place, but there is also death."

there's nowhere else to go. The place where they have one of those pie and pastie hot counters where the pastry goes dark and forms little heaps and the fossilised savouries are like shrivelled relics that have been in Tiverton forever and will continue until long after you and I are dead and departed from this funny world.

But just on the edge of town comes the biggest surprise of all, the canal. It still has a horse drawn barge working it, although I'm never sure if this is a tourist attraction or just a lack of progress. Nevertheless, as you escape suburbia the old cut quickly transforms into the most beautiful little rustic waterway you ever laid eyes on. Cute and clear and decked out with fleets of perfect lily pads. In the summer at least.

January is crueller. A thinner, more sinister charm. Dead reeds, naked trees and pike. "Pike" sounds inadequate in fact, like we were just talking about one. Earlier in the year you can see them everywhere. Pike on bends and straights, pike under trees and bushes, pike sitting in weedy bays and under boats, pike lying there like dead wood, fast asleep, pike prowling about and looking for trouble, pike lying next to bigger pike and hoping they don't notice. Local myths aside, many of these savage natives are little longer than a school ruler. But beautiful all the same these finely painted little murderers. On some days you can throw a spinner or a fly just about anywhere and carnage erupts. But today the only thing that is just about anywhere you look is ice. Sodding miles of the stuff. So I decide to walk.

The water in the little village of Halberton is solid. The boat pool resembles some kind of crude experiment where local kids have tested this magical new medium by hurling everything and anything they can find across it. There are rocks and sticks, a plank of wood and even a dead rat lying prostrate. Swans and ducks slide and skate awkwardly on the surface, stepping around stranded projectiles, wondering what happened to the water. Worse, some evil trickster has slid a few tempting silver coins onto the ice like some form of peasant trap.

Enclosed under this frozen top sheet is another, separate and trapped world. Below the surface, life continues and where there is less carnage, the ice forms a great window you can peer through. Several little perch sit on the bottom like resting sparrows. A shoal of roach hurry past. Looking deeper, towards the centre of the pool you can spot sleepy looking bream, their languid backs cold and still.

The frosts lend a certain beauty to the place, but there is also death. Further along the bank are two small, very dead roach, stuck fast in the glazed surface of the canal. And yet something has to profit from death, if I could only find just one clear spot. Just one gap is all that's needed, I'm thinking. Just one little gap in the ice, even if it's only wide enough to drop a dead bait. And that's when I picture it in my head—the side stream a mile or so further on where flowing water just might provide an area of clear, non-frozen canal.

The little inflow is there just as I remember it, creating a corridor of open water that looks almost black next to the ice. It's a fantastically shadowy few metres of canal. A gentle swing and the dead roach drops neatly into the hole, the red top of the float siding after it before sitting upright.

Calm resumes and all you can hear is the trickling inflow. The surrounding canal looks impossibly shallow and derelict. The banks are scolded, just straw coloured stubble replacing the waist high growth of the summer. Gone too are the summer visitors. An old half-stray dog used to haunt the banks here and gratefully accept scraps. Has winter stolen you too?

As I resolve to give it a last ten minutes, something finally stirs. The float shudders just once before ever so gently the tip saunters sideways almost drunkenly. Line passes smoothly downwards until I lift the rod smartly.

There is no sudden burst of violence, just a creeping presence. Strange sensations follow as braided line meets ice. Once the fish wakes up and accelerates there is an eerie splitting, cracking, clicking sound. A great piece of ice is cut clear like a crooked pane of glass. The fight doesn't last long. The pike wallows as I turn it towards me and plunge the landing net into freezing water.

Along with the catch, clear splinters and broken fragments lie scattered in the net. It's a slight miracle, this green and gold pike of perhaps five pounds. The fish lies so still that for a few odd seconds it resembles a model, smashed out of a glass case. Moments later she swims off sleepily like it never happened. Cracked islands of ice litter the canal. ●

THE PROFESSOR AND THE PIKE

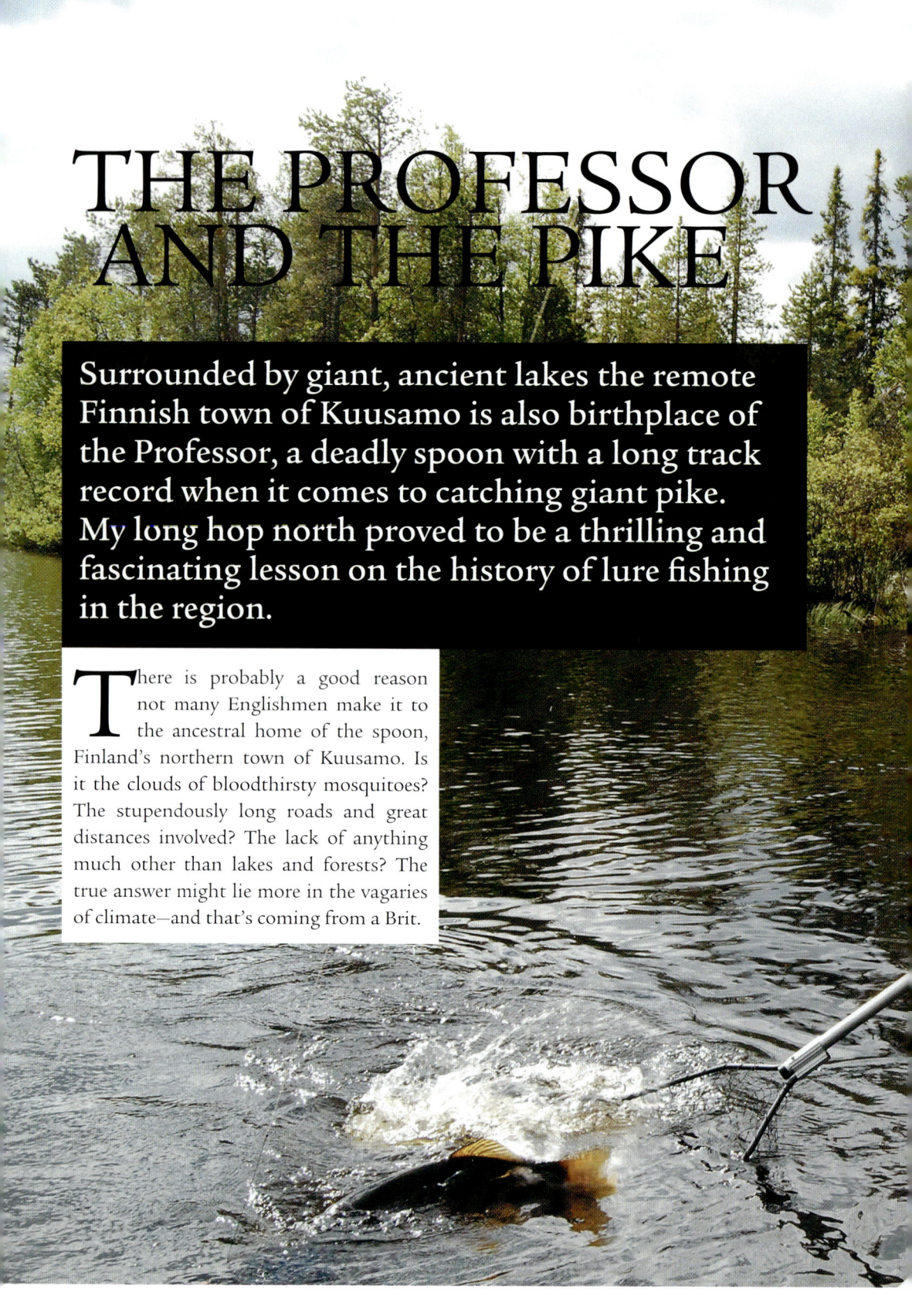

Surrounded by giant, ancient lakes the remote Finnish town of Kuusamo is also birthplace of the Professor, a deadly spoon with a long track record when it comes to catching giant pike. My long hop north proved to be a thrilling and fascinating lesson on the history of lure fishing in the region.

There is probably a good reason not many Englishmen make it to the ancestral home of the spoon, Finland's northern town of Kuusamo. Is it the clouds of bloodthirsty mosquitoes? The stupendously long roads and great distances involved? The lack of anything much other than lakes and forests? The true answer might lie more in the vagaries of climate—and that's coming from a Brit.

Tangles with Pike 43

THE PROFESSOR AND THE PIKE

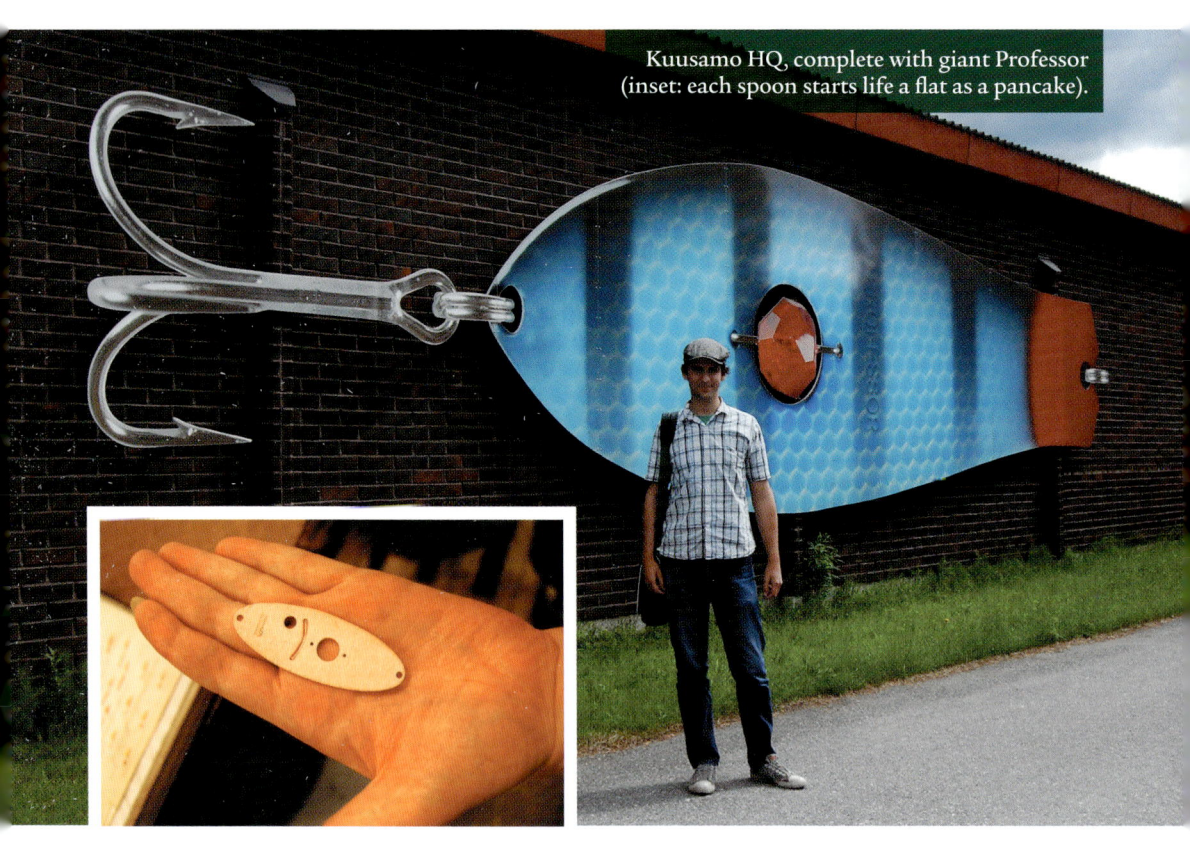

Kuusamo HQ, complete with giant Professor (inset: each spoon starts life a flat as a pancake).

"All our lures are made to catch fish," explains Kimmo, "but sadly the fish don't have any money so we must appeal to anglers too."

"It is quite early for pike, I must say" comes the crackle of Kuusamo boss Kimmo Korpua over the phone. A bit early? It's late May. "We have a late spring here," he continues, "two weeks ago there was still ice on most lakes."

Nevertheless, I'm not put off. Besides the hundreds of crystal clear waters, Lapland is a place of rich fishing history. On the long road north, you can tell that this is a nation with angling in the blood. The average supermarket here has more lures than a typical UK tackle shop. Not that there are many up north, you understand. Even so, it is a region where the sparse population of locals still rely on fishing and still rely on traditional craftsmanship. Roadside garages display local specials—hand carved concoctions of wood and metal, meticulously painted creations from the functional to the outlandish.

The Kuusamo lure headquarters itself is hard to miss—a gigantic spoon hovers on the side of the building as I meet the boss, a tough looking bloke who oversees the production of some 700,000 lures each year. At the visitors centre I'm given a brief but enlightening education in the history of the spoon.

"These lures have a long history in the region," he explains. "Local history shows that

44   Tangles with Pike

KIMMO'S TOP 6 SPOONS (OPPOSITE)
1. Professor 00 (190mm/60g perch/ gold). A big spoon for a big appetite! A great option for large waters.
2. Professor 0 (150mm/40g silver/ copper). Long casting, big pike favourite with EU anglers for over twenty years.
3. Weedless Professor 1H (115/36g perch/gold). Where weed makes fishing difficult, this model keeps catching.
4. Räsänen (90mm/28g black, gold & silver). A highly effective spring and summer spoon with a tighter action for active pike.
5. Räsänen (70mm/20g silver & orange). Finland's best selling spoon is a great all rounder for various species.
6. Fat Professor "Onega Special" (90mm/30g blue, red, white & silver). Wide profile and a lovely, loose wobble make this one deadly at slow speeds. Great for shallow water.

spoon-type lures have existed for around 4000 years." These were originally made of bone, with other early models cut directly from the sides of copper pots, the curved metal shape providing movement and flash. From these simple roots, the Finns refined today's spoons over centuries. Mass production only came far later with the advent of factories and precision metal cutting and finishing. The famous Professor was first registered in 1927.

Having fled England for a spell with headlines of European recession and the rise of cheap far Eastern labour in the background, the operation at Kuusamo somehow defies the times. The company relies not on space-age technology but the input of a relatively small number of expert lure makers. Kimmo insists: "We will never do things cheap and compromise quality. Yes times are not easy, but fishermen trust what we make."

In a world where successful designs are often shamelessly copied, this represents a genuine challenge. Kimmo has even seen Chinese imitations as flat as pancakes! It's perhaps no coincidence that in some areas of the factory I'm not allowed to take pictures- the process of getting the exact curve and finish witnessed in these classic spoons is a jealously guarded secret.

Nevertheless, a walk through the making of a spoon proves fascinating. Each comes from a flat strip of top grade copper or brass. They are cut to shape, with a telltale hole in the middle. The spoon is then curved to an exact shape, before the metal is treated and hand polished to a deadly, dazzling shine.

The other unique feature of a Kuusamo spoon is the hole and red glass bead, which acts as a target point and also helps the lure flutter enticingly on the drop. The classic silver and gold spoons still work a treat, but others are coloured on one side. A perch pattern serves as a good example of the typical process, in this case using eight separate steps of adding colours and scale patterns. Every lure is hand sprayed and finished.

A question pops into my head that I can't resist asking: Are all these sexy finishes aimed at the fish or the fisherman?

"All our lures are made to catch fish," says Kimmo, "but sadly the fish have no money so we must appeal to anglers too."

A LECTURE ON A LAKE

Of all the places I've ever cast a line for pike, the Muojarvi, a vast and stupendously clear lake, is one of the most beautiful I have ever seen. There are vast open spaces of sparkling water, along with giant bays festooned with rocks and reeds. One month ago, an ice drill would have been necessary to do any fishing. Today we will take a boat and search the shallows. Spoons can be trolled, but it's much more fun to drift and cast.

The "little bay" Kimmo advises we try first turns out to be as wide as a football pitch, a broad finger of rippling water that looks as likely as anywhere to test some old and new Finnish specials.

The easiest way to use a Kuusamo, or indeed any spoon, is to simply crank at a regular pace to get an even, fluttering and wobbling action. A quality spoon will also work at quite slow speeds. Alternatively, by livening things up with a little twitch or faster turn on the reel, the spoon becomes slightly more erratic. A less well-known fact about the Professor is that the hook can be switched to the other end of the lure; back to front you get a different, alternative wobbling action. Kimmo

"The 'little bay' Kimmo advises we try first turns out to be as wide as a football pitch."

recommends a lively style for active pike and milder temperatures while slowing down to a lazier sink and draw method for cooler water when the fish are lying on the bottom.

The lures look devilishly attractive even with the most basic of steady retrieves, but this is by no means the only way to operate. As Kimmo explains, the Finns use a range of presentations from trolling to vertical jigging through the ice. I'm especially intrigued by the flash and fluttering action created by presenting the spoon "on the drop," and this is another way to catch. Fishing "sink and draw" works especially well with a big, meaty professor, in a manner not too dissimilar to how you might present a wobbled dead bait. The spoon can be allowed to sink to the depths, before being drawn upwards, then paused, and so on. Today however, the fish should be up for a chase, having woken up nicely from a very long winter.

You hear plenty of lure anglers say that colour is of little importance, but not Kimmo. In the more coloured southern Finnish lakes, he asserts, bold and dark colours can be very useful. Here in the pure waters of the north, lighter natural finishes such as the perch colour or a simple copper or silver spoon often work best. Even so, we decide to switch colours until the hits arrive.

Perhaps tellingly, the first take I receive is virtually on the drop. I make a long throw towards the reeds and allow the spoon to flutter downwards in around six feet of water. One turn of the reel and something murders it, the rod hooping over. After some hectic moments of manic power, a deliciously marked pike of dark green and gold comes to the boat. More soon follow—or perhaps this is the wrong word because they don't tend to follow the spoon at all but simply beat the hell out of it. Time and again, it seems that a little pause thrown in does the trick, a pike grabbing hold as the lure wobbles forward again after a brief stutter.

On our sunny Lapland morning, a silver and orange spattered model does most of the damage. It's a variant that has already won a recent pike tournament in southern Finland and quickly becomes my new favourite lure. It doesn't take me long to suggest that Kimmo produces some of the magnum-sized professors in this colour. A new secret weapon perhaps?

"You shouldn't keep any successful lure secret!" Kimmo implores me. "If it works well you should always tell people. That way we will make more of them." He recounts that in the past that some of the deadliest "secret" patterns never got a long enough run in production, partly because those in the know didn't publicise their worth.

The action continues with the best pike of the session hitting the lure in a brutal rush. She does her best to return the spoon in mid-air, but my luck holds and Kimmo sinks the net. "Not bad" he nods. It's a good double, but who knows what might be lurking in this vast, unspoiled habitat? As well as roach and perch, the resident pike have ide, trout, whitefish and even salmon to feed on.

The comedy moment of the day arrives when Kimmo snags a well tooth-marked Professor on the rocks, before we spend anxious moments turning the boat to retrieve it.

THE PROFESSOR AND THE PIKE

"The action continues with the best pike of the session hitting the lure in a brutal rush. She does her best to return the spoon in mid-air, but my luck holds and Kimmo sinks the net."

"Does it really matter?" I ask. "You make thousands of the bloody things." He winces as he tries to cajole it free. "I know, but this is one of my favourites. I've had him for ages."

HAPPY RETURNS

Aside from the great lakes of Finland, the Professor is equally no stranger to British shores, with a number of lunking great specimen pike to its name. Aside from the tempting, wallowing action of a large spoon the other real plus point is how well they cast. The slim profile allows a spoon to literally "cut" through wind, a feature appreciated by Brits tackling large expanses of windy water from lochs to reservoirs.

In my own fishing, I can vouch for their effectiveness on lakes such as gravel pits, even in pretty unpleasant conditions. After the Finnish experience I'm also now inclined to try fishing them slower in sink and draw fashion in the cold, rather than automatically reaching for the dead baits.

Other venues also suit the spoon. They work well in flowing water whether cast upstream or downstream, and the smaller Kuusamo Rasanen tempts trout and perch as well as pike.

Where the conventional spoons are somewhat less effective is on weedy, narrow water such as a drain or canal. In this case, a weedless model takes some beating—but it is a shame that the UK angler has such a poor choice of models in comparison to other parts of Europe. Nevertheless, if you shop around weedless hooks are available which can be swapped for the usual trebles without killing that tell-tale flutter.

Naturally, the folks at Kuusamo balked when I suggested that you might "improve" a spoon by combining it with rubber, a suggestion akin to adding ketchup to a meal prepared by a Michelin star chef. But this is another trick I like to pull. Provided you use only a small, grub style worm or similar soft plastic the action should be undiminished- and I do like the extra wiggle, for perch and zander especially. Just don't tell the Finns.

A spoon may not seem like the obvious choice given today's vast array of rubber and plastic lures then, but I still know one or two old heads who swear by the flash and swerve of a meaty spoon. And why indeed not? In a climate where every year brings a new range of passing fads, here is a thoroughbred that has caught big pike and evolved over four millennia. ●

Kuusamo Spoons. Although you'll find the professor at some of the main predator tackle retailers, some models can be harder to find. Perhaps the best UK selection can be found at www.friendlyfisherman.co.uk or try: www.lureshop.eu

For more on Kuusamo Lures and the visitors centre: www.kuusamo-finland.com

Ollilan Outdoor Adventures: Slap bang on the shores of the Muojarvi, where we fished, Ollilan offer accommodation near Kuusamo from just 350 Euros a week, boat included. For the huge size of the lakes, angling pressure is light and this would be an ideal base for a visit. See: www.ollilanlomamajat.fi/en/

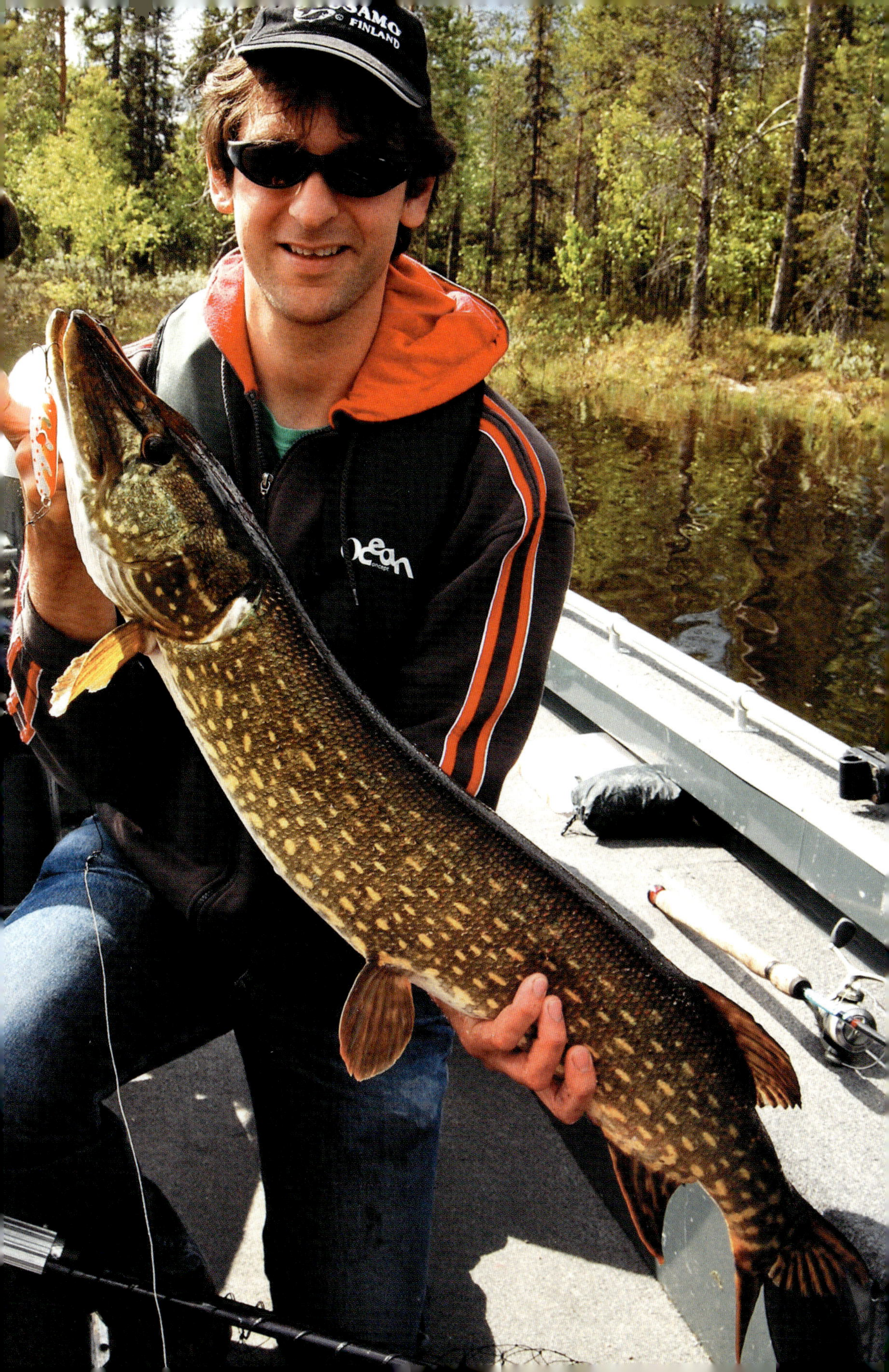
KUUSAMO FINLAND
ocean

CHEWED OFF

It might be easy to imagine the capture of large pike on a trout water to be a piece of cake. The reality on Chew is more often a case of blind hope, mislaid plans and KGB style surveillance.

You've heard the lines one hundred times before about Chew Valley Lake. Some love it, some hate it. Plenty of others both love and hate it. As sure as night becomes day the stories arrive every season: "Huge Pike from Chew". The captor's fish of a lifetime is then roundly credited and slagged off, quite often in the same sentence, by the hundreds if not thousands who wish they had caught it.

Has any other venue ever made such mixed press? Here is a water named a "circus", "a lottery" and virtually in the same breath "a mecca for big pike". My own feelings are equally mixed. Casting a big fly on a mild spring afternoon can be utterly fantastic. On a windy, bitter day in the infamous "Pike Trials" it can be mind-alteringly bad.

Perhaps it is not the place itself then, but the constant scrum of anglers that colour my perceptions. The set up itself is a little weird and frantic in the first place. Once upon a time you wrote them an old fashioned letter to get into the trial, and when they had received more written pleas than Father Christmas, names were then picked at random. Latterly, I am informed, it is more like phoning the constantly engaged hotline for a gig you suspect has already sold out.

On only three occasions have I been lucky, or unlucky, enough to fish the trials. The lodge at Chew on these mornings resembles an airport departure lounge for pike anglers: A collection of hairy blokes with their scattered coffee cups and coloured maps. And always one imbecile you wish would take up golf, who seems to have a vocabulary almost exclusively based on the words "twenty", "thirty" and "f***."

Out on the lake itself, all is fairly quickly forgiven because the place is undeniably beautiful. It is an enormous stretch of open water along with various sizeable, named bays

CHEWED OFF

Happier returns: A hopeful spring session with the fly rod.

that the faithful pin their hopes on like long-shot horses in some obscure race. A whole armada of pike anglers then start motors and head out in different directions, some of them going straight to the spot where yesterdays big one was caught, others according to their own random calculations.

Each day begins with logic and good intentions, before the warmth of the lodge is a distant memory and the contestants resort to prayers, curses and skullduggery. The most essential items tend not to be herrings or special rigs, but fish-finders, mobile phones and the dreaded binoculars. You can expect constant text updates from your boat partner's mate, along with KGB-style observation from neighbouring boats every time a fish is hooked.

At first I didn't believe the stories of surveillance, but the first Chew pike I ever hooked was carefully watched through lenses from the next three boats. At about four pounds they quickly lost interest, in contrast to the poor sod who caught something six times bigger and suddenly found his patch invaded by an entire raiding party.

Is it cricket? Nobody seems to give much of a toss as long as they get a crack at the big one. And this is largely what is wrong with the size obsession of modern piking: it turns nice guys into monsters and friends into bitter rivals. Statistics tend to do this to anglers. The reports tally up amazing counts of twenties, thirties and even more vast fish, but what they don't reveal are the thousands of hours, casts and baits that led to these monsters. Nevertheless, it's fair

52   Tangles with Pike

to say that anglers thrive not on certainty, but possibility. The thought that the very next bite could be an insanely big fish is enough to cause pike men to lose sleep the night before, and drive cars from the opposite end of the country fairly rattling with tackle.

You can feel expectations shift as the day wears on. In the first hour or two everyone is talking about lake records. By lunchtime, a twenty would wrap things up nicely. If you're still struggling by last knockings you would just like to remember what a pike actually looks like. I never did manage a monster in my three trials days and the heaviest catch I made was a muddy, broken umbrella. In actual fact, I found the frost-bitten humour, fried breakfasts and the scenery the most enjoyable parts of the experience.

I wish I could tell you how I soldiered on and used my skill and determination to catch a vast Chew fish. But the truth is, I left the place well alone. After all, there are waters that are just as beautiful and inviting. They might not have quite the same enormous pike, but they also lack the crowds of anglers, high costs and constant wagging of tongues.

It was only a couple of seasons later that I really became enamored with Chew in fact. Nor was it a bitterly cold winters day but a pleasant trip in May with my friend Steve Moore, whose enthusiasm sparked my own. On arrival a miracle seemed to have taken place. Fishing minus five layers and a hat was liberating for one thing, and with only a handful of boats out the whole atmosphere had changed.

> "I saw a huge head break the surface, jaws open and with an almighty shake the fly was thrown clear. The line went limp and I felt slightly sick."

All geared up to cast giant flies, it was Steve that issued the priceless advice of trying smaller, subtler patterns. And what a glorious afternoon it was, drifting in the sun and waves and teasing the pike. I'd caught two outrageously fit double figure pike on my own black pike flies, before I hooked that "bloody hell" fish. It was as powerful as an oil company. Yard after yard of fly line disappeared and still I had no sight of her. I'm convinced that Steve jinxed the whole operation as we caught a first glimpse and he announced: "now that's a twenty." I saw a huge head break the surface, jaws open and with an almighty shake the fly was thrown clear. The line went limp and I felt slightly sick.

After that day, Chew became an occasional flirtation rather than a dedicated campaign. I had little desire to go for the trials but perhaps a couple of times each season I would go and enjoy the place, as often as not with a trout fly rod as well as the nine weight. Even so, a big lost fish is something that can haunt you. This is the double-edged sword of a place like Chew. It's easy to say it doesn't matter, but in the back of your mind you start to wonder when exactly the next chance will arise.

Over a handful of sessions, I arrived with the bit between my teeth but left nonplussed. There was the day it resembled a churning sea of dark, fishless water. There was also the time I watched a fish of at least a metre long seize my boat partner Pete Wilkins' fly, but somehow fail to get hooked. It was only a whole season later that an invitation from the Angling Trust's Paul Sharman triggered my desire to get even.

Anglers often talk about that instinctive gut feeling they get that "today will be the day." Meeting Paul at the lodge I didn't have even a whiff of it. Few pike of any description had been caught lately. The lake looked placidly indifferent and I had almost resigned myself to the fact it would be a pleasant social, rather than an outstanding session. A reasonable day to take your girlfriend out for a picnic on the boat if nothing else, and I smiled when my other half Paulina said: "Who knows, maybe I'll bring you some luck?"

Can an angler try too hard? I suspect there could be some truth in this. If you're in too much of a rush to succeed, it can indeed affect your fishing. You hurry your fly or lure in too quickly or move spots too soon. But how different the mood was on this occasion as the three of us drank in the sunshine and chatted away while the boat drifted and we made our casts.

While Paul had a handful of takes and two fish, I received just one touch all day. But perhaps "touch" doesn't come close. In one of the far corners of the lake, I was idly watching my roach-styled fly return to the boat when I witnessed a hulking shape make a sudden lunge. As the rod flexed hard over and my heart started to thump, there were immediate echoes of that previous lost monster. "You're going to lose it!" teased the voice in my head. I decided to underplay the thing to my companions: "Could be a decent one this," I ventured.

One thing you cannot deny about the "plastic" trout-fattened pike of chew is that they fight like demons. Possibly it is the typically shallow water that encourages them to take off on long, nerve-shredding runs. For perhaps three or four half-horrible, half-exhilarating minutes, the thing was possessed. This time however, as I managed to wrestle her to the surface I gave the fish no time to shake out a barbless fly. Into the net went twenty-one pounds of sheer relief. The pike may have gone mad, but I had just got even.

Will I be there in a phone queue, crossing everything in the hope of a ticket for the trials this winter? I think I could recreate the experience in my back garden by sitting on a heap of ice while burning fifty quid and getting people to spy on me while relaying messages about some lucky bugger's fish of a lifetime caught miles away. But give me a call on a decent spring day when the circus has left town and the binoculars have been put away and you might just tempt me back. ●

MURDER BY NIGHT

Although only something the experienced and well-prepared angler should take on, the odd night session can add extra excitement to your pike fishing.

It's already getting dim by the time we near the water. Street lights flicker on above the bridge, the sun is gone and in no time the day fizzles out with all the subtlety of a power cut. The idle flow of the river runs black beneath us. Dead leaves drift and the natives are restlessly heading home or filing into the pubs on the Quay. And here we sit, thawing out herrings and thinking of pike.

"Hey mate, what are you doing?" comes the call from a random observer. The fishing rods should make it obvious, but it's a question I've already asked myself. Pike fishing is a sport for frosty mornings, surely? But you already know the score: most of us are in no position to nip to the river whenever the mood takes us. That four-letter word, work, has other designs for most anglers.

Nevertheless, evening sessions that run right into the black of the night can be a decent time to target pike. They don't simply disappear in the dark. On the contrary, they can be surprisingly active. A healthy sized lure or potent smelling dead bait is still easily located by a lurking pike. In any case, it certainly beats sitting through the bullshit of midweek TV.

Provided you're well prepared, the experience can be a highly enjoyable one. There's something about the darkness that makes the exercise even more charged with sinister mystery than before. Even the waters of a humdrum urban river seem loaded with veiled menace as it gets properly dark.

Night piking is no operation to be approached casually however. Everything becomes twice as awkward in the dark and

Tangles with Pike 57

you simply cannot go about the task without a measure of careful planning. Besides warm clothing you need sensitive bite indication that will work in pitch-black conditions. Glowing floats or indicators and bite alarms are sensible steps. Equally imperative is a head torch, not only to find your way around, but also to leave you with both hands free to handle and unhook pike safely.

INTO THE BLACK
The orange glow of a bobbing night float is a delightful sight on dark waters. Along with my long suffering angling mate Norbert Darby, we drop float-legered baits into a deep hole in the river. Experience from roach fishing days tells me that this little corner, on a slight bend in the river, has no shortage of prey. But where are the pike?

The stretch is not noted for specimens and poaching has been a worrying recent trend. Few club members seem to fish here, but perhaps on those grounds it's time we reclaimed the stretch from the menace of poachers. In spite of the occasional set line or fish theft however, I'm not deterred. The fish are still here, there are simply too many deep holes and hidden snags for it to be any other way.

An hour gone and the only interest has been from a group of lads on their way to the pub. As with the local football team, it seems even the most casual observer always has a self-proclaimed expertise when it comes to fishing. Seeing as there are half a dozen of them and they all have haircuts shorter than a match head, I don't feel like arguing. Yes Sirs, there is nothing to catch here—you are right, you are clearly experts and what tasteful tattoos you have. Now please kindly piss off.

Thankfully they do just that and the evening draws on and falls into a languid

MURDER BY NIGHT

> "The thing creeps ominously away from us across the flow. Jumping up to grab the rod, I strike hard and feel an eerie, lumbering presence on the line."

state approaching peace. Norbert suddenly remembers that he hasn't had any tea. I watch his rod and ten minutes later he returns with a tin of cider and a packet of crisps. Meanwhile, we're accosted by an old upper crust gent walking his dog. He recalls tales of fishing from Scotland to Africa using even worse language than the young hoodlums who came by earlier. Which is all very entertaining, but I'd swap all of his tales for just one solid bite.

I am a restless angler in truth, not good at sitting still for indeterminate shifts. And so I try to fidget productively. As well as freshening up my bait, I like to chop the old ones into pieces and throw these in. If nothing else, it keeps my hopes up.

The bait has only been back in the water for five minutes when Norbert announces- "I think your float just moved." I study the orange tip again, which continues to sway gently in the flow. I'm about to put the claim down to cider and poor lighting, when the thing creeps ominously away from us across the flow. Jumping up to grab the rod, I strike hard and feel an eerie, lumbering presence on the line.

The pike stays deep and lazy, only displaying something approaching fireworks as the pressure is increased. Slowly but surely I manage to guide her upwards until the beam of the head torch captures a gaping, angular head. The final few seconds are like slow motion, waiting for a last thrash that never quite arrives. I'm relieved that Norbert has only had the one cider and is fully switched on as he sinks the net well under her.

The pike is magnificently long and fiercely marked. It feels weird holding her up for a picture in the glow of one of the streetlights behind, an unhooking mat protecting the fish from a concrete path. Some passers by have already come for a look, but this is no time to oblige curiosity and after quickly weighing her she's promptly returned.

No further runs develop, but I sit on my perch beside the railings a whole lot more contented. Half of me wonders why I don't do this a little more often when short daylight hours and work threaten. Looking down the river, there must be a dozen tempting spots within half a mile. And while they might produce in the day, there is a definite sinister charm to a spot of night fishing. ●

THE UGLY DUCKLING

Of all the various ways I've caught pike, using replica birds and water rats must rank among the weirdest. Disappearing ducklings set the wheels in motion for a deranged little project.

"I've seen it with my own eyes," the old lady told me. At first I didn't know whether to simply dismiss her as a local nutter. "Horrible" was the word she used to describe possibly my favourite living creature. "Every year we see the little ones dragged under," she went on. "I hope you catch those nasty pike and get rid of them." I couldn't help but chuckle, which was perhaps not quite the expected response. Then again, some pathetically small broods of ducklings on the canal had me thinking she may have a case after all.

I was about to explain to the old dear that such attacks were only natural—a cruel but necessary link in a food chain which certainly wasn't designed by Walt Disney. But I spared her that lecture and instead, my brain began ticking over with strange, gruesome possibilities.

A duckling live bait was too savage to contemplate even for my die-hard pike angler's sensibilities. But what about a specially made imatation? I had caught plenty of pike on surface popping lures, rubber frogs and all sorts of other strange creature replicas. Why not a duckling? The fact that I'd never seen such a lure only seemed to add to the temptation.

I've made mayflies and midges, wooden plugs and even mouse style lures in my angling life, but a duckling was a fresh challenge. My workbench quickly became cluttered with eyes and feathers, felt, fur and tools. A body of balsa or foam could be easily shaped and weighted to land right side up. Coloured flock produced a lovely, lifelike finish. Other details were less than essential but hard to resist- including two cute eyes, a beak and even a pair of webbed feet made from leather. A perfect little ducky—although I hoped the poor little critter might not look so tidy for long.

TIME FOR A SWIM

Play began on a misty morning tossing the "ugly duckling" along reed lines and into the weedier parts on the cut. An early start seemed a good idea if only to avoid the ridicule of being spotted by locals taking a replica duckling for a swim. It was no pike which reacted first but a brown mallard with her own brood, pushing forward and quacking loudly at my little imposter. Quite a weird sight, but I'm told mother ducks will angrily drive away other birds, even other birds' ducklings.

It was to be some time before I could

persuade a pike to respond with the same enthusiasm, well beyond the point after which I'd asked myself "have you totally lost the plot?" Lure fishing is always a test of character when biteless spells occur, but when you're carrying out an altogether more far fetched experiment the mind games get more pronounced. And yet I was sure the pike must be responsible for a few disappearances.

Joining the ducklings were fluffy gray moorhen and coot chicks. If nothing else I was determined to make a convincing impression of the real birds on the water, trying to provide a series of nervous bobbing motions, with little hurried bursts perhaps suggesting a straggler separated from its family. The more unhinged part of my mind began to imagine the possibility of a whole team of lure anglers working together to give the illusion of an entire brood of ducklings—with one designated nutter using jerkbait tackle to play the role of "mother". If anyone fancies trying this, you'll find me in an institution somewhere in Devon.

I was just about ready to give up and slip on something more sensible when it happened. The thing materialised from nowhere, the canal changing from placid to panic in a heart beat. No ceremony or warning—just a sudden rush and the duckling was gone, only rocking water in its place! Anticipating the mother of all pike I was a bit surprised to find the culprit a greedy jack of no more than four

Tangles with Pike   61

pounds. No matter, there was the duckling sandwiched between its jaws, tooth-pocked and missing an eye. The plan had worked! I began to laugh a little hysterically. Not for the first time in the day, the passing dog walkers eyed me like I was on drugs.

DEATH AT THE SURFACE
Further experiments ensued with the creation of more home spun surface lures. Looking at successful surface lures and pike flies from my past, the successful candidates often seemed to be those with a high disturbance factor. I wish I could tell you that the perfect looking duckling produced for this article was fantastically successful. The truth is, it wasn't. Later, scruffier models seemed to work way better. As with the flies anglers tie, messy but mobile often out-fishes carbon copy realism.

A change of plan was thus in order and besides ducklings, those scruffy moorhen chicks seemed perhaps even more suitable to imitate. And so the next lures made were a messier mix of fur and feathers. Water rats are another favourite and I still have the picture of a spring seventeen-pounder taken on a mouse I'd fashioned out of balsa and fur, the only major elaboration being half a shoe lace for a tail. The other big clue looking back at this picture from the late nineties however, is the abundance of weed. Surface fishing only seemed to kick off when the stuff grew back with a vengeance. The pike definitely appeared more willing to smash at a surface lure through suitable cover. The flipside was that getting them out proved tougher, calling for strong-arm tactics and tough, dependable tackle. On many occasions I would wade up to my waist in duckweed infested margin to net a fish.

Back to the drawing board though, and I returned a little later to a now weedier canal. Every few yards along the bank saw the lure land with a slap onto the water, little trails developing on the scummy surface. New lilies were already up in force. As well as coot chicks I saw a swimming grass snake. The place had come alive, I felt sure something had to happen.

There is a certain obscene pleasure in watching a little fledging, especially a pretend one, pulverized in a sudden moment of violence. And to be the one pulling the string is like being involved in a sort of puppet show for maniacs. Exciting isn't the word.

Exciting maybe, but another aspect of surface fishing is the frustrating regularity of takes that are missed. Only after several wild hit and run attacks with the new prototype did I get something to hang on properly. "Unceremonious" is hardly the word for the manner in which a good-sized pike grabs its' victim. Less rush was involved this time as I watched a large head break through the weedy surface and murder the sorry little bird. The pike exploded as contact was made, downing a dozen young lilies as she went. Praise the Lord for 40lb braid is all I can say. Seconds later she was wrenched into the net, weed and all. And there in her jaws was the bizarre sight of my furred and feathered lure, perhaps not such a crazy idea after all? ●

Homemade surface lures of different guises.

Tangles with Pike

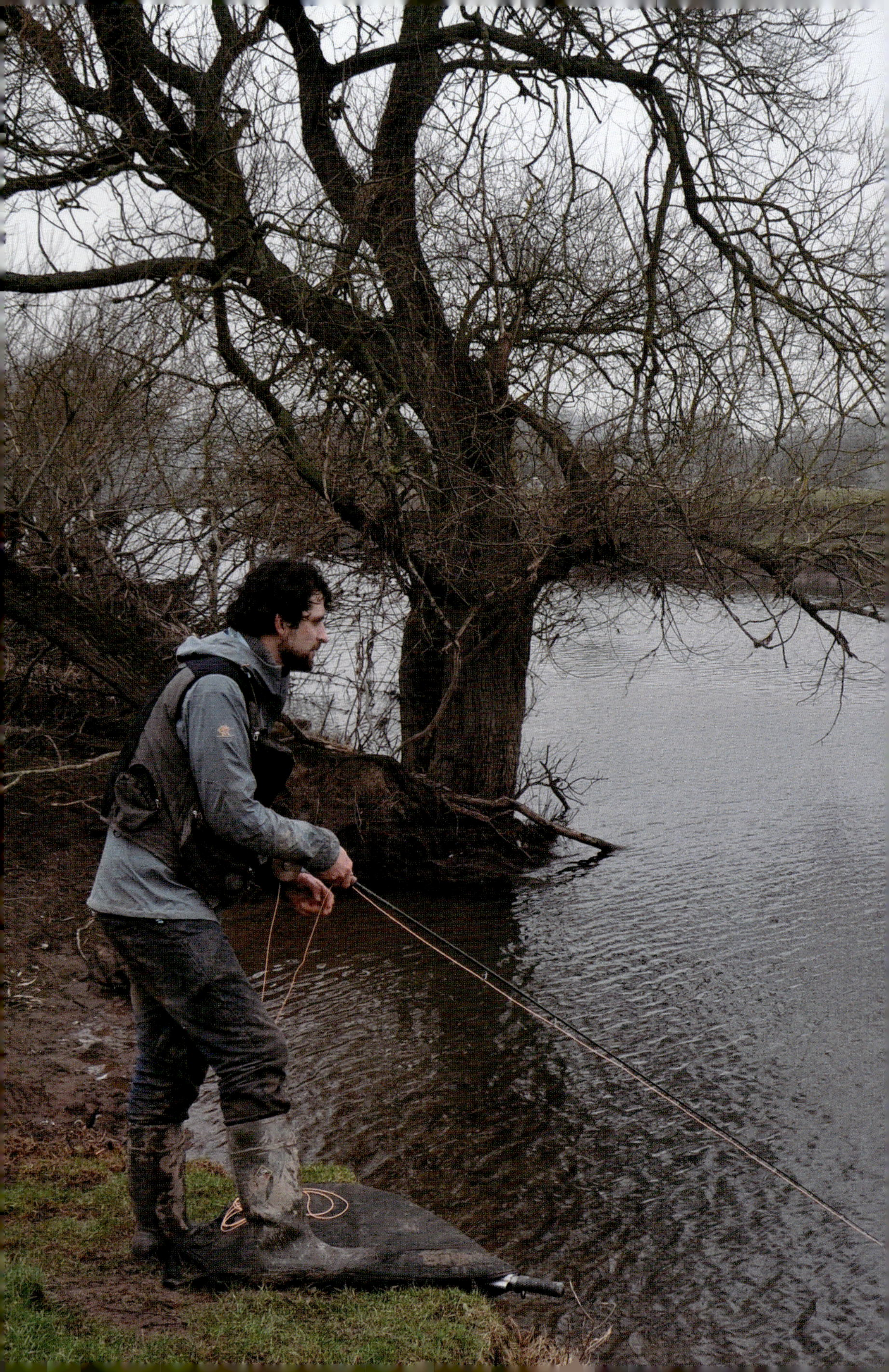

REVENGE ON THE WYE

A moody monster of a river, the Wye is a destination that can test any angler's patience. What keeps dragging you back? The thought that everything can change in just one cast.

Is there a more formidable, changeable river in Britain than the Wye? One day you could happily wade across parts of it, the next you'd need stilts or a death wish. Depending on the season, you could approach it with the most slender trout rod or tackle bordering on sea fishing gear.

On a good day it looks fabulous. We've all seen the pictures of big fish and sunny, settled waters. This in a sense is part of the torture. Angling features tend to give us the final result: a grinning angler, a big fish, a bit of shameless tackle promotion. Seldom do you get the hard lessons, and in my case the thorough kicking that paved the way.

What it is with the Wye? I'm not sure. Had my timing simply been off? Perhaps. To call this famous river fickle is an understatement. Because the Wye encompasses such a huge stretch, it takes water from a vast area of soggy hills and mountains. And while you might plan as carefully as you like, the practise is rarely quite as straightforward as the theory.

If the River Wye were a human being, it would have a bi-polar disorder: massive spells of gloom and dank flooding, interspersed with fantastic highs in which anything seems possible. It's the possibility of the latter scenario that keeps you coming back for more.

TURBULENT TRIPS

My introduction to the Wye came almost by accident a few years ago. I'd been travelling

> "Again, we return to that gulf between the grinning idiot in the fishing catalogue, and the real and altogether longer, muddier process of trial and error."

further afield with my brother in search of grayling and trout fishing. One look at some of the meaty bends and monstrous slacks on the river was all it took to turn my thoughts to pike.

Perhaps the Wye has a great record for pike because there is simply too much of it to get clobbered by anglers. For the record, some of the stretches way upstream offer amongst the most underexploited pike fishing of all. But I've struggled here if I'm honest. The pike are not numerous when coarse species thin out—but they have a massive amount of grayling and trout to eat, to say nothing of their habit of polishing off dying, spawned out salmon.

My first taste of pike came in a typical hot spot lower on the river—a huge slack where the Wye's dramatic flooding had caused entire sections of bank to cave in. While sections like this on my local rivers might be only small pockets, on the Wye they can be enormous. Such obvious, gnarly locations appeal to the angler's primal imagination. They just scream pike. In times of prolonged flooding, the pike stack up in such areas. They have little choice when flows are violent and in the resulting groupings of fish, small pike disappear to make the females even fatter. In fact I've seldom caught many jacks on the Wye and the bigger fish almost always look well fed.

Tackling up in itself can be a rude awakening. Granted, you might get away with a simple float or leger rig in a sheltered spot. For the rest of the time however, the tackle is off the scale: two ounce floats, strong braid and substantial pike rods can often be essential to negotiate deep, powerful water. Regular flooding also deposits horrendous amounts of debris and heavy float leger rigs incorporating a weak link to the weight are common practise.

My first successes were in giant semi-slack areas off the main body of the river. I recall trips with dirty water and endless crap sticking to the line; but also frosty mornings where the runs came quickly and I had low doubles along with the promise of more.

One very important lesson I've learned in the process is to avoid being too footloose. Yes, there are many tempting bits of river. But unless you're lucky, you'll only reap the rewards from a particular area by getting to know it better. Sometimes that means blank, exploratory days or long walks where notes are made for future reference. Again, we return to that gulf between the grinning idiot in the fishing catalogue, and the real and altogether longer, muddier process of trial and error.

DRIFTWOOD AND DISASTER

Perhaps the ideal situation for a Wye angler is the freedom to be on the water at short notice. I'm well aware many of us don't have such license. But the problem is that if you book a ticket and accommodation well in advance, there's no guarantee whatsoever that you'll hit the river when it's productive—or even fishable.

Flood water fishing is something I've succeeded with at home, but seldom got right on the Wye. One spot, a slack the size of a small lake, looked ideal for a high water mission. Even in chest waders however, it turned out to be not only debris strewn but dangerous. The waders were required just to get through the fields.

Other aborted missions had been just as

REVENGE ON THE WYE

day fee of £15 it isn't the cheapest piking, but not bad at all considering the fact you'll almost certainly have a beautiful section of water all to yourself. There is also a one rod rule however. With fair walks sometimes involved though, you might be grateful that you travelled light.

HAPPY RETURNS

Do you ever get the feeling a place has it in for you? I had my suspicions on a late raid last season. I had permission to fish from some promising looking farmland rented by a friend, but that was about where my luck seemed to finish. After a week of settled weather, the dark gray was coming. Roads were closed everywhere. I had arguments with the satnav, then with maps, and then a collapsed bridge, finally making it to the river rather down in the mouth.

Of all the slacks I've fished on the Wye however, the one beyond the cow fields I discovered must surely have been the most tempting I'd ever seen. With the rain already starting to spatter I feared the worst, before looking into the water. It was clear. Bloody clear. Off the scale in terms of the Wye in the back end of winter.

Regardless of venue these days, fantastically clear water has the same affect on me: I reached for the fly rod, digging out some large patterns that had worked well on other formidably large rivers. My usual pike fly rod was set up with a fast sink tip, before the 20lb fluorocarbon and wire trace, to get the fly exploring well down in the deep depression in front of me.

With grim determination, I fished the sixty yard slack like a salmon angler in search of a single take, taking a step and a cast at a time and letting the fly sink deep. Fly fishing is not a great method of determining depths, but

frustrating. On one occasion I had a passable first days fishing, before the rain well and truly set in. The next day, looking out of the window the scene was unrecognisable. The river had come up a full six or more feet. Seeing me a little crest-fallen at breakfast, the hotel owner suggested I could fish just outside his gardens in a little flooded channel where he'd taken chub before. It would have been a great back up plan, had I got a single run.

On this point, it's worth mentioning that the river is dotted with hotels and B&Bs. Many places with accommodation also own water and so it can be worth staying at different locations—all it takes is a friendly word and you might uncover some hardly touched pike fishing. In fact, so much water is only normally fished for other species.

The more usual channel is the Wye and Usk Foundation's booking scheme. With a typical

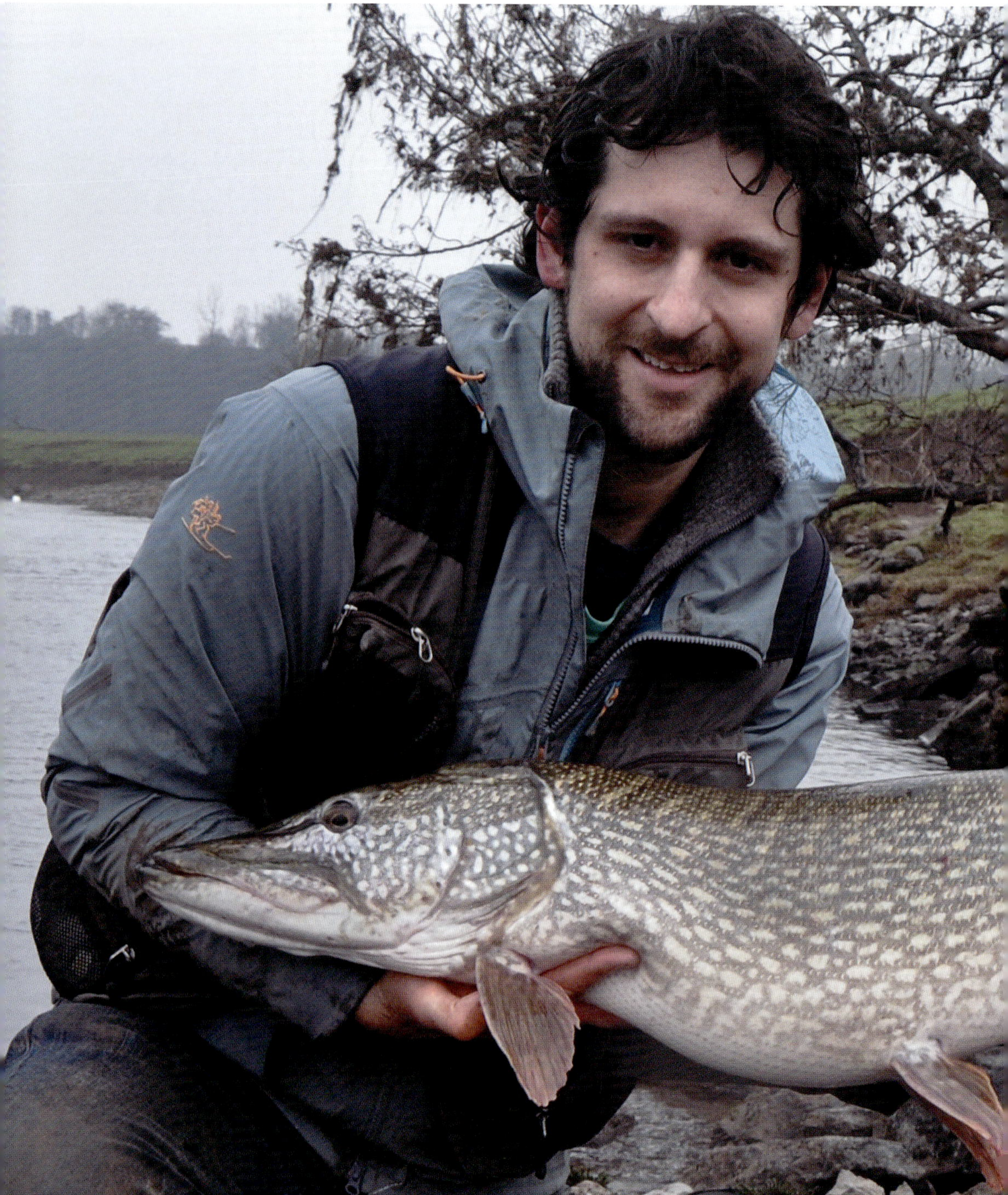

with a simple count down each cast you get a feel for a swim. Once you begin snagging debris, it's time to count less or speed up the retrieve slightly.

My confidence as an angler has always been a bit like the River Wye itself—above head height one day, painfully low the next. But even as the casts added up, the clarity of the water was spellbinding that day.

About an hour into the session, with the bay shallowing up I finally got my touch. A single, solid tap. The sudden transformation from dead weight to gut wrenching power was terrifying! Part of me thought I'd fluked a big salmon, the way the fish pelted downstream. But she stayed low and moody. Every time I managed to gain a few feet of line back, out the fish flew and again and the rod creaked.

The worst part of the whole process was the netting. By God was the swim nasty! I'd managed to walk parallel to the fish, but the bank was like bloody quicksand. As she came up, my wellies went down and down into the clay. I pictured the farmer coming down to the river later to discover just my boots wedged into the dirt.

With the fish safely netted at the edge I had to haul my footwear clear, before clambering to a safer area to weigh and release her. What can I say? Anglers tend to speak of their joy or satisfaction at "the big one." Personally, I find that sheer relief comes long before any such feelings. The numbers mean little. Twenty-four pounds and an ounce is at best a poor way to sum up that Wye fish. It isn't a photo opportunity or bragging rights, but a sense of kicking back and overcoming the odds. In the space of a few hours I'd been despondent, doubtful, exhilarated, drained and ecstatic. Such is the Wye. The mud and the blanks can be hellish, but revenge doesn't get much sweeter. ●

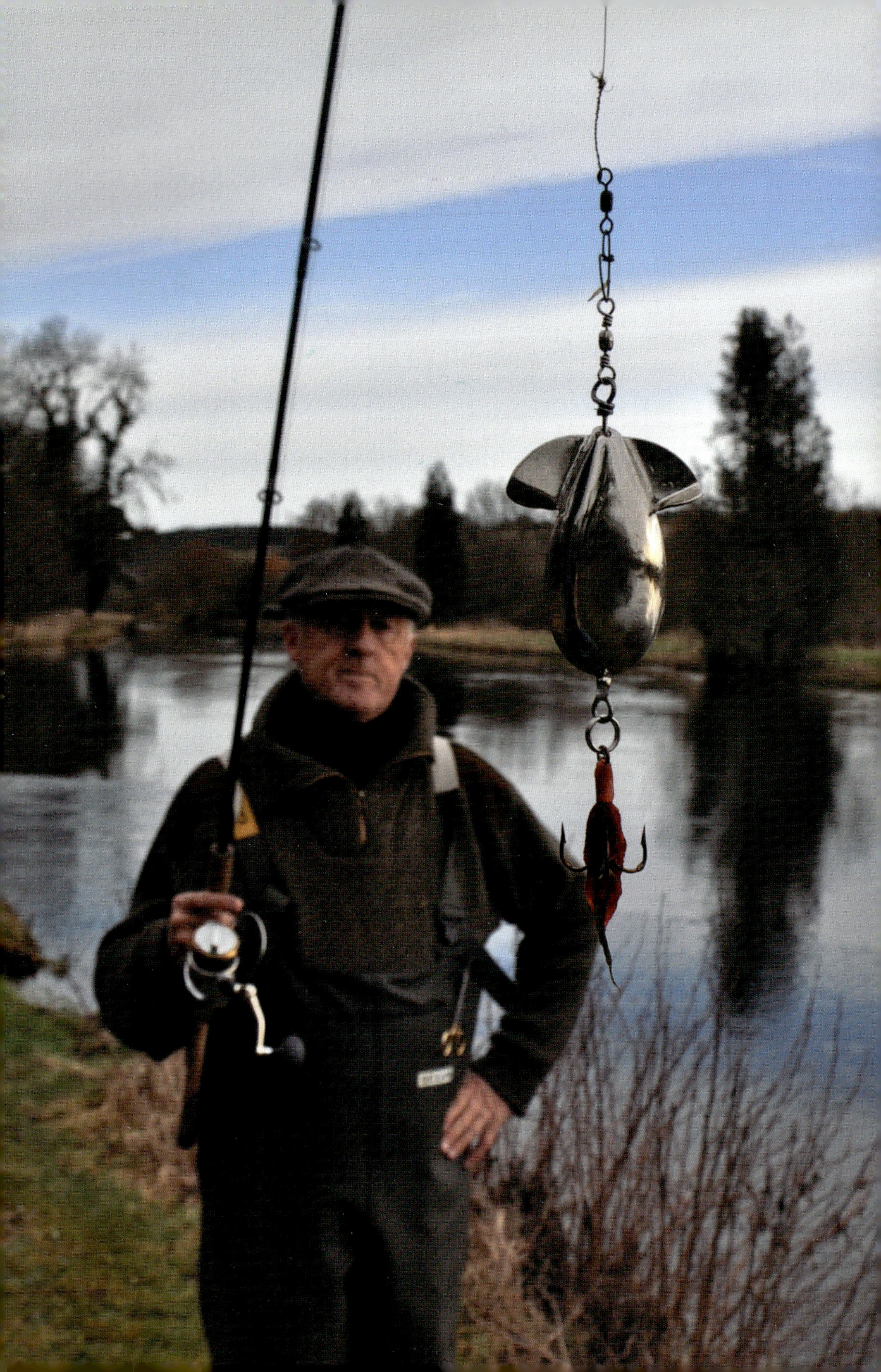

TARRANT VS. TEETH

Lifelong angler Chris Tarrant may have fished all over the world, but is still simply nuts about pike. I met him on an unlikely stretch of chalk stream in search of a monster.

If you were to hazard a guess at the kind of fishing TV stars and celebrities prefer, you might quickly draw up a very exclusive shortlist of species. A spot of salmon fishing perhaps? A quick hop to the Florida Keys? Chris Tarrant has experienced many destinations, but still gets some of his greatest kicks from the pike, a fish he has pursued since childhood.

"For me, it all started fishing with my Dad on the Thames," he recalls. "Pike have always excited me. When you're a kid it's the big, scary fish, the one with the teeth. We used to use bleak under a float." Back in those days, Chris might have caught the pike fishing bug, but landed no monsters. "The biggest one I saw was not much above ten pounds, a fish which my dad—bless him—managed to knock off at the net!"

On today's outing the quarry might be the same, but the setting is idyllic by comparison as we tackle up on a stretch of the Test. "The chalkstreams can be such good fishing," he says, "much of the water is hardly pike fished." In the bad old days, pike were treated as vermin—but thankfully some of today's river keepers are more enlightened. "Some people still think that pike eat all the trout—but in reality they're far more interested in roach and coarse fish. If anything they keep the average size of the trout higher," he remarks. The culling of pike is one of his pet hates: "On one lake I know they killed a thirty-eight pounder!" he remembers. "And yet you rarely hear about trout found inside pike that were gutted. What's wrong with these people?"

As we sort out our tackle, he's joined by

> "There are swirling eddies, sinister slacks and classic reed lines galore. While Chris brings his Colorado spoon fluttering to life, I cast a hand sized pike fly across the current, both of us hoping for a big hit."

fishing pal of many years Bob James, who'll be fishing for grayling today. "Before you ask Chris, no—I'm not donating any big grayling as bait!" he warns. If Bob's kit is a model of slightly obsessive order, Chris has an approach closer to my own—a bag a bag that is full of random odds and ends. He quickly finds what he wants though, a lovely old-fashioned Colorado spoon.

"John Horsey put me onto these at Chew," he says. "A lot of folks have switched to soft baits, but these things are still great. Some days you just can't fish them too quickly. You're there reeling the thing back hard and —BANG—they really hit 'em."

We take a roving approach to the mile or so of water we've been given permission to try. Much of the year this is game fishing only, although it looks lovely for pike. There are swirling eddies, sinister slacks and classic reed lines galore. While Chris brings his Colorado spoon fluttering to life, I cast a hand sized pike fly across the current, both of us hoping for a big hit.

Before the sun gets up higher and hotter it's a pretty fresh morning, but Chris is undeterred. "My biggest ever pike came on one of the coldest days I've ever fished," he explains. That specimen, a Chew thirty pounder, tops off some excellent sport on the venue for Chris. "It's unreal," he says. "I've fished some great pike waters, like Llandegfedd and Ardingly. But they tend to go downhill pretty quickly. The Chew fish just get bigger, and the trout fishing can be top class too."

This is all well and good, but we're starting to wonder if there are any pike in today's

TARRANT VS. TEETH

A big pike in the company of Bernard Venables: "One of those crazy days you never forget!"

stretch of water. A few casts later and we have our first answer as a frightening looking bow wave forms after Chris's spoon. "Come on you beauty," he begs, "come to Chris!" Sadly the fish gives up the chase. "Don't you just hate it when you run out of water?" he sighs.

I'm quite happy pausing with the net ready, but Chris is curious to see if the fish might prefer something else. "Go on, have a cast—see if he'll take a fly." Two shots later and my eight weight is wrestled over with a bang. It's not exactly the Terror of the Test, but a fit and exquisitely marked six-pounder.

As far as flyfishing for pike goes, Chris is very much among the converted. Indeed, a day of hectic action on Chew with guide John Horsey will form part of a mini fishing series to be aired later this year. "It's absolutely brilliant fun," he enthuses. Even some of his more old school fishing friends have caught the bug it seems, such as fly fishing expert Mike Daunt. "He's one of those great characters," says Chris, "he's fished for trout all his life and yet is now obsessed with pike. When we turn up at a new water, all he wants to know is if there are any pike."

Does Chris have a favourite predator fishing destination I wonder? "Anywhere but here," he jokes, shooting a critical glance at Bob James. "I thought you said there were pike here Bob? This place is rubbish."

74 Tangles with Pike

> **"A frightening looking bow wave forms after Chris's spoon. 'Come on you beauty,' he begs, 'come to Chris!' Sadly the fish gives up the chase. 'Don't you just hate it when you run out of water?' he sighs."**

"I blame the angler," replies Bob, who is already seeing some action from grayling, and duly promises to give us a shout if any fish are stolen on the way to the net.

The predator venues Chris has fished would form a long list. "I used to love piking in Ireland," he reflects. "There were so many pike and you never knew what you were going to pick up, it could be a jack or a twenty on any cast. Sadly it's just not quite the same any more." He is critical of culls and netting policies in particular. "They just don't seem to understand that live pike are a big asset to tourism," he says. "Just look at the income Chew generates. Pike are definitely undervalued."

As for most memorable days on the bank, Chris has fished alongside some of the biggest characters in the sport—from Eddie Turner to Neville Fickling. One of his greatest ever

TARRANT VS. TEETH

sessions was the capture of an upper twenty on the Hampshire Avon—and he still has a picture of the fish, along with an unexpected guest in the form of Bernard Venables, "just one of those crazy days you never forget," as he describes it.

Chris has fished as far afield as Canada for pike and muskies, but still thinks the fishing in Britain is worth shouting about. "Terry Eustace got me into piking on the Wye and it was probably the best pike fishing I'd ever had," he recounts. "It's still pretty good, and

> "For one of the biggest names in TV and radio for several decades, time on the bank means more than just catching fish."

Chris grimaces at the memory. "Bloody hell that hurt! The ghillie started pulling and I just said 'no you don't!' You get that sick feeling. Not good."

The next bite is once again on the fly, and for a few seconds of comically choice language our famous angler changes from Chris Tarrant to a character closer to Roger Mellie, the Man on the Telly. "You lucky basket!" he grins. "They definitely want the fly today."

Whether the sport is good or indifferent though, I get the feeling that for one of the biggest names in TV and radio for several decades, time on the bank means more than just catching fish. His has been a wide-ranging career, but perhaps he doesn't envy the lot of those whose focus is always on fishing TV programs. "The fishing bits on film I've done were great fun, but I wouldn't like to do it all the time," he remarks. "It can be tough. Once you start worrying about whether you catch fish or not—well, that's not really why I go fishing."

As the light starts to go he takes as much interest in a circling barn owl as I do to squeezing in a handful of "last" casts. As we reluctantly break down our rods and call it a day, he sums up close of play on the river perfectly: "There's no such thing as a bad day's fishing—especially when it takes you somewhere as beautiful as this." ●

with such a head of coarse fish, salmon and trout there's always the potential for big pike."

As for less delightful fishing memories, the next anecdote reminds me to watch my backcast. "I hooked myself in the back of the head with a big tube fly on the Tay once."

PIKE FISHING IN SUSPENSE

From multiple treble hooks to gags, pike fishing has had various ideas from the dark ages to overcome. But just how much have we moved on in terms of bait presentation? It might defy convention, but you'll often catch more pike by looking higher in the water, whether that means drifting, suspending or even trotting baits.

Why is it that some ideas in fishing survive for so long unchallenged? Dead baiting has been a Great British tradition for centuries, but as well as a highly effective method we are left with a helping of dogma The Vatican would be proud of.

Take our deadliest ambush predator, a killer that loves to rush upwards to seize its prey from below and what do we do? Plonk a dead fish on the deck, below its eye level. If you think I'm being flippant, just look at the pike's head: the eyes are positioned high, to focus forward and upwards; the mouth is slightly underslung. This is not a creature that feeds like a barbel.

Part of our stubbornness in changing habits is perhaps down to sheer laziness. It's easier to drop a bait on the deck and leave it alone than let it drift in the breeze or current, giving our full attention. We also have the idea fixed in our heads that two or three rods are better than one, a habit that not only limits our mobility but leads to more deep-hooked pike.

So why not change the rules a little? It might mean fighting your instincts and old

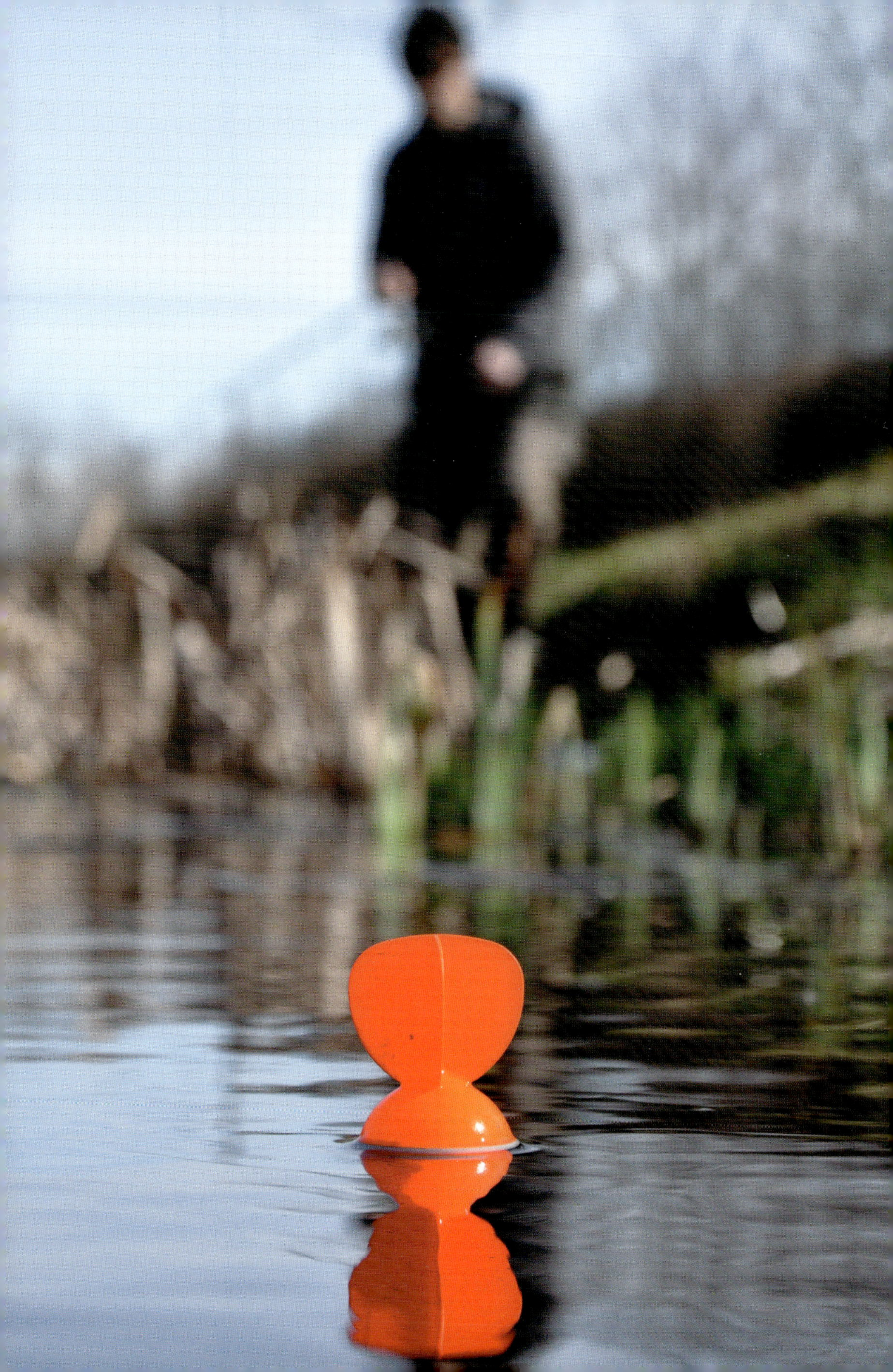

habits, but float fishing dead baits clear of the bottom has several major advantages. Firstly, we can use the elements to our advantage. Whether it's the current of a river, the tow on a canal or drain, or just the breeze pushing across a stillwater, we can search a heck of a lot of water. In the autumn, when flows become festooned with debris, this is a particular advantage because you don't have a fixed line continually trapping dead leaves and bits of weed. Nor will your bait ever get buried on the riverbed where it can't easily be found.

A suspended bait is also a dynamic method that gives the pike a simple "take it or leave it" decision to make. Predators hate the feeling that lunch is about to disappear, hence you'll often get a quicker response than with a bait just sitting dormant. Takes are often spectacularly positive too. With the bait off the bottom, that sudden flurry of jaws is registered immediately. The pop of the float can only mean one thing and you'll never be left in any doubt as to whether to strike, which is thrilling stuff but also better for the pike.

ALL SET FOR SUSPENSE

Drifting or trotting a dead bait under a float is a one rod operation ninety percent of the time. I cannot stress highly enough the value of holding the rod and giving the process your full attention. For this reason I don't like a beast of a pike rod and reel, much preferring something like a light carp rod and mid-sized reel loaded with strong floating braid. A fixed spool is easiest, but I do also love using a centrepin for smaller rivers and drains. Call me eccentric, but

> "We have the idea fixed in our heads that two or three rods are better than one, a habit that not only limits our mobility but leads to more deep-hooked pike."

nothing gives better control over a bait trotting down in the current- and that applies to a dead smelt as well as bread flake.

A float taking 20-30g of weight is usually just right on rivers, drains and canals. I like a model with a fairly chunky, highly visible profile and those with dart flights are also great for picking up a little extra movement from the breeze.

My rigs also differ from standard traces in that I often only use one treble hook, usually a size four. This is nicked through the back of a small to medium dead bait, so that our offering sits upright in the water. I like smaller baits for a couple of reasons. Firstly, large baits can be clumsy to cast and come adrift more easily. Second, smaller offerings are easily devoured by even a modest pike, which means I can strike instantly and avoid the risk of bait and hooks being swallowed. One semi-barbless treble is so much kinder to the pike than two.

Typical dead baits are smelt, sprats and small roach. Where long casts are not required I like the sea baits because they will come off on the strike, leaving the hook clear to make its mark. For longer distances, coarse fish provide a tougher alternative. I'm also a big fan of dying baits. I once considered this a gimmick, but having tried them extensively on waters with less than great visibility I now swear by an added dash of colour.

SEEK AND DESTROY

The process of searching the water with a suspended bait is hardly rocket science, but does demand your concentration and a little thought. I would usually start by presenting the bait at a midpoint in the depth (for example, at three feet deep in six feet of water), experimenting and altering this if I'm not getting bites.

A smooth side cast is generally the preferred option to keep bait intact. The bail arm is then kept open, but with the index finger dabbing the spool to carefully control how much line is paid out. Drifting along the near bank is easy. Letting the bait trip along the opposite side of a drain or river can be trickier, but the best way is to let a bow of line form so that the tow or current takes the bait along parallel to the far bank. This can be a deadly way to let your dead bait saunter along the far shelf of a waterway—but you must be quick to take up the slack and strike when a bite occurs. I much prefer braided line these days for a clean strike and the extra strength.

Don't assume the trick only works on waters that flow or tow however. It has worked well for me on breezy lakes and gravel pits too, and I find a scaled down set up far more manageable and enjoyable than using those huge traditional drifter floats.

Perhaps the biggest obstacle to success is simply the angler's mindset that bait belongs on the bottom. But pike have no objection to snatching fish in midwater, whether alive or dead. In fact the method is also a viable alternative to live baiting, a method which is not only now illegal in many places but one so many of us have mixed feelings about.

The choice is yours then, but for that next roving pike trip why not take just the one rod and try something different? You'll cover far more pike than you would with several rods just sat on your backside and I can assure you, the suspense is deadly. ●

PIKE FISHING IN SUSPENSE

This double figure fish took a roach dead bait presented well off the bottom.

PIKE FISHING IN SUSPENSE

ESOX AND THE CITY

The natives may be restless and the scenery grey, but urban settings can provide some surprisingly good pike fishing.

Ask most pike anglers about the kind of places they love to spend time and you'll quickly get a picture of reed lined lakes, quiet rivers and drains. Certainly not the local city centre with its endless traffic, assorted rubbish and the occasional passing alcoholic. With their street lights and concrete embankments it becomes difficult to imagine what many of our urban rivers once looked like. You might readily assume that a great deal of these places are almost lifeless, choked by our own greying development. And as often as not, you would be quite wrong.

The quality of fishing can be the last reason why anglers avoid urban waters. It is more to do with a lack of privacy and natural beauty, not to mention the potential danger of some

PIKE FISHING IN SUSPENSE

of our more "lively" urban areas. Exactly how unsafe or indeed unproductive it is to fish these places, however, is often wildly different from our own assumptions.

The simple fact remains that fish populations can and do thrive surprisingly well in towns and cities. Indeed, there is something of a contradiction at play where you find vast concentrations of people and yet relatively few anglers. The fish themselves can be in good condition as well as fair numbers too. Piking aside, perhaps my most memorable evidence on this score has been catching some beautiful trout with a fly rod on a stream cutting right through an industrial estate. On deeper, grander rivers I've seen salmon leaping beneath office buildings, while pike and perch and indeed most other species of coarse fish also exist undetected. Appearances can and often are deceptive, as the urban angler finds out.

OUT ON THE TOWN

Urban fishing undoubtedly brings its own challenges and requirements, but our first priority should be safety. Evenings and night times are undoubtedly the most dangerous time to venture forth- but whatever time you decide to fish, it is good practise to keep in company where undesirables may lurk. Tackle should be kept to a minimum and always tidy for the same reason. This is not paranoia but basic common sense. For example, on one recent urban trip one track-suited lad spent about half an hour loitering where I was fishing with a friend. As police walked the other bank he took a sudden interest in fishing, using us as cover!

On other visits, groups of townies on the booze have been another issue with predictably stupid or plain offensive comments. In either case, you simply must keep level headed- watch your back, keep a low profile and you are usually quite safe. If you are especially anxious about your local patch however, early mornings are generally a more peaceful time.

For all of the technical complexities we bring to our pike fishing the initial battle remains the same in urban fishing as anywhere else you cast a line: find your fish. Where concrete uniformity seems to smother everything, the importance of any features whatsoever is magnified. Bridges, quays, side streams, weirs and bends are all worthy of investigation. Even in the most dull looking water however, there will be hot spots and points of interest only discovered if you look.

Initial trips to any urban water should be mobile affairs and several ways of feature finding exist. A simple walk with polarizing glasses is well worth the effort when you find a river or canal painfully low or clear. Fish finders such as the Smartcast are another obvious way to chart depths and areas of interest. However, I much prefer simply prospecting with lure fishing tackle. I like a fairly fast sinking rubber jig for this business,

Single hook jigs are ideal for searching urban waters—and less heart breaking to lose than expensive plugs.

> **"Your aim should be to slowly build a mental map of surroundings and this includes potentially dangerous snags such as the obligatory shopping trolley—local hooligans are so unimaginative these days."**

which can simply be counted down to various depths. A single upturned hook is ideal for these snaggy waters and if you couple this with strong braid you can even save tackle and littering by simply straightening hooks on more gruesome snags. I could write an entire article on local oddities found, including traffic cones, a radiator, an old fashioned telephone and entire submerged bicycles. Fellow Westcountry piker Steve Moore once hooked and landed a soggy trainer, before making it a matching pair a few casts later! In short, you might find just about anything besides what you were actually looking for.

Braid gives a terrific "feel" for exploratory work too and your aim should be to slowly build a mental map of surroundings and this includes potentially dangerous snags such as the obligatory shopping trolley (local hooligans are so unimaginative these days). Of course, lure fishing also brings the added advantage that you may well catch fish while sussing out the water, immediately telling you which areas may be worth a return.

Human activity also has its bearing on fish activity. Areas where birds are fed are a classic in towns, drawing in silver fish and hence also predators. Bridges are another common gathering area and sanctuary for small fish, while the deep water and shelter of boat yards makes these areas come into their own during winter floods. The nearness of buildings, factories or indeed any man made structure could indicate sheltered, slightly warmer water which can mean concentrations of fish throughout the winter. At other times however, the holding areas will be far less obvious— perhaps just a little extra depth or weed.

Hot spots are a curious subject in themselves. On my own local waters I've found that anglers tend to congregate in one or two productive, convenient areas but leave many other less obvious, less accessible or highly public areas well alone. Flood arms

PIKE FISHING IN SUSPENSE

> "Anglers tend to congregate in productive, convenient areas but leave many other less obvious, less accessible or highly public areas well alone."

The author makes the most of a quick stop in Rotterdam.

and areas near pubs are typical city hot spots—productive, but the pike are warier and often in poorer condition. Sadly not all who fish these spots are careful with their catch and awkward swims of concrete steps and railings take their toll. The irony is that on other areas of the same river you might find some of the best looking pike you've ever laid eyes on, in complete defiance of their surroundings. My own captures and those of friends on a single river simultaneously show some badly damaged pike which seem to get caught time and again, but also some very healthy fish which look like they've never seen a hook. Have a wild guess at which areas yield the battered specimens?

CONDITIONS DICTATE METHODS

Uniform they may appear, but urban waters are as changeable as those in more idyllic areas. It should go without saying, but we should always fish according to the factors and conditions found on the day rather than our own preferences. Lure fishing is a classic example—very useful when the river is settled or fining down, but near useless when the water is high and coloured. I would love to bring a fly rod on almost every trip—fantastic when clarity is good but pure futility on a flooded water. On shallow, urban canals, for example, I sometimes manage a couple of hours settled fly fishing in the early morning before boat traffic churns things up and out come the herrings.

Your actual rigs will often also be dictated by factors beyond your control. Float fishing quickly becomes impractical, for example, if the water is regularly used by boats and rowers. The latter have that annoying habit of travelling backwards with no awareness of your position. Confrontation is no solution though and you can either reel in every ten minutes whilst turning the air blue, or adapt. Much of the time legering is vital in city

A nice fly caught fish from the town. Don't leave home without the unhooking mat!

centres—with your rods angled downwards, tips under the water if necessary to avoid both boat traffic and also swans and other birds. Water birds can be a particular menace in urban areas as they often show a total lack of fear where they are fed on a daily basis. If banks are hard you may also need to bring a rod pod, although this carries the obvious risk of being mistaken for a carp angler.

Again, it is important to remember that however grey your city waters look, fish respond to changing conditions just as they do in a more wild setting. Low water levels and mild conditions, for example, may see the fish congregate near weirs and other well oxygenated places. At the other end of the scale, floods bring about an even more drastic change but are perhaps the conditions most needlessly feared by anglers. In fact, high water levels can concentrate the fish to an uncanny degree and in suitable slacks and sheltered areas you can really reap the rewards. It also seems that this is the time when "bonus" unknown pike from other areas may travel fair distances for food and shelter and in fact when the water is at its muddiest and ugliest is perhaps your greatest chance of a genuine surprise.

THE STINK OF THE CITY

Perhaps the real draw with urban fishing is thus its propensity to throw up unexpected results—there is almost a reverse psychology

> **"Floods bring about drastic change but are perhaps the conditions most needlessly feared by anglers. In fact, high water levels can concentrate the fish to an uncanny degree."**

at play whereby busy waterways become neglected by anglers as fewer people are prepared to fish them and hence they possess a far more limited track record. Naturally, there's no smoke without fire and sadly there are factors which some may find off-putting.

Certain unavoidable issues directly affect fishing in the town. There may be no suitable place for bank sticks let alone a place to park your backside, whilst concrete is bad news for landing fish and you should never, ever be without an unhooking mat—which also doubles up as somewhere to stow stray items of tackle or sit on.

Another obvious factor are other bank users. One of my worst angling memories occurred when I was the victim of an unprovoked assault by a pair of yobs on a bank holiday some years back. It says it all that these young "men" decided to attack someone not even looking in their direction. Thankfully, what they didn't realise was that my older brother was further down the bank to even things up and we put one of those neanderthals in hospital while the other got a lift to the police station. While I refuse to change my habits for the benefit of imbeciles, certain times are well worth avoiding around the rougher city pubs.

City anglers themselves are often a haphazard crew. In the absence of many "serious" types you may well find local kids fishing with crude tackle. My answer to this is always the same: speak to them and be civilized. You may be the only example they have to follow. Where fishing is so utterly public it is never truer that we are all ambassadors for our sport. It says a great deal about our media that we are taught to habitually fear and condemn others—but be civil to those you encounter however, and the vast majority of people will respond positively. Remember, these places belong to everyone. This is not necessarily a negative factor and I'm sure I'm not the only one who has enjoyed some fascinating, quite accidental conversations with local characters whilst fishing in public places.

In fact, for all of my own "beautiful fish in beautiful places" ethos, I find searching the more industrial looking parts of our landscape an exciting alternative prospect. There is certainly something strangely thrilling about catching fish from a dead looking water. The possibilities are out there if you are brave enough to look.

Convenient, predictable fishing it certainly isn't and whether it's a pack of local kids asking random questions, listening to the philosophy of passing lunatics or the bizarre, impromptu gathering of onlookers who watch as you play a fish, urban fishing is always a colourful experience. And while I am well aware that there are some dodgy places involved, look beyond the tabloid headlines and you'll find our towns and cities are still vibrant places. Runners and rowers, drunks and shoppers are all part of this urban landscape, so why not anglers too? There's only one way to discover just what might await in the waters of your own town, right on your doorstep. Just don't be too surprised if you get more than you bargained for. ●

ADVENTURES IN LAKELAND

With stunning scenery, strange sights and more pike infested waters than you can shake a rod at, Finland is a fabulous destination for pike fishing.

"So remind again which lake this is?" I'm looking at the outstretched map, looking for a clue but struggling to place the broad sweep of water before us. You might think someone had spilled liquid onto the page, such is the patchwork flood of blue. The shapes are anything but uniform. There are vast, rocky seas and little wooded tarns; lakes shaped like tear drops and others that cross the map like

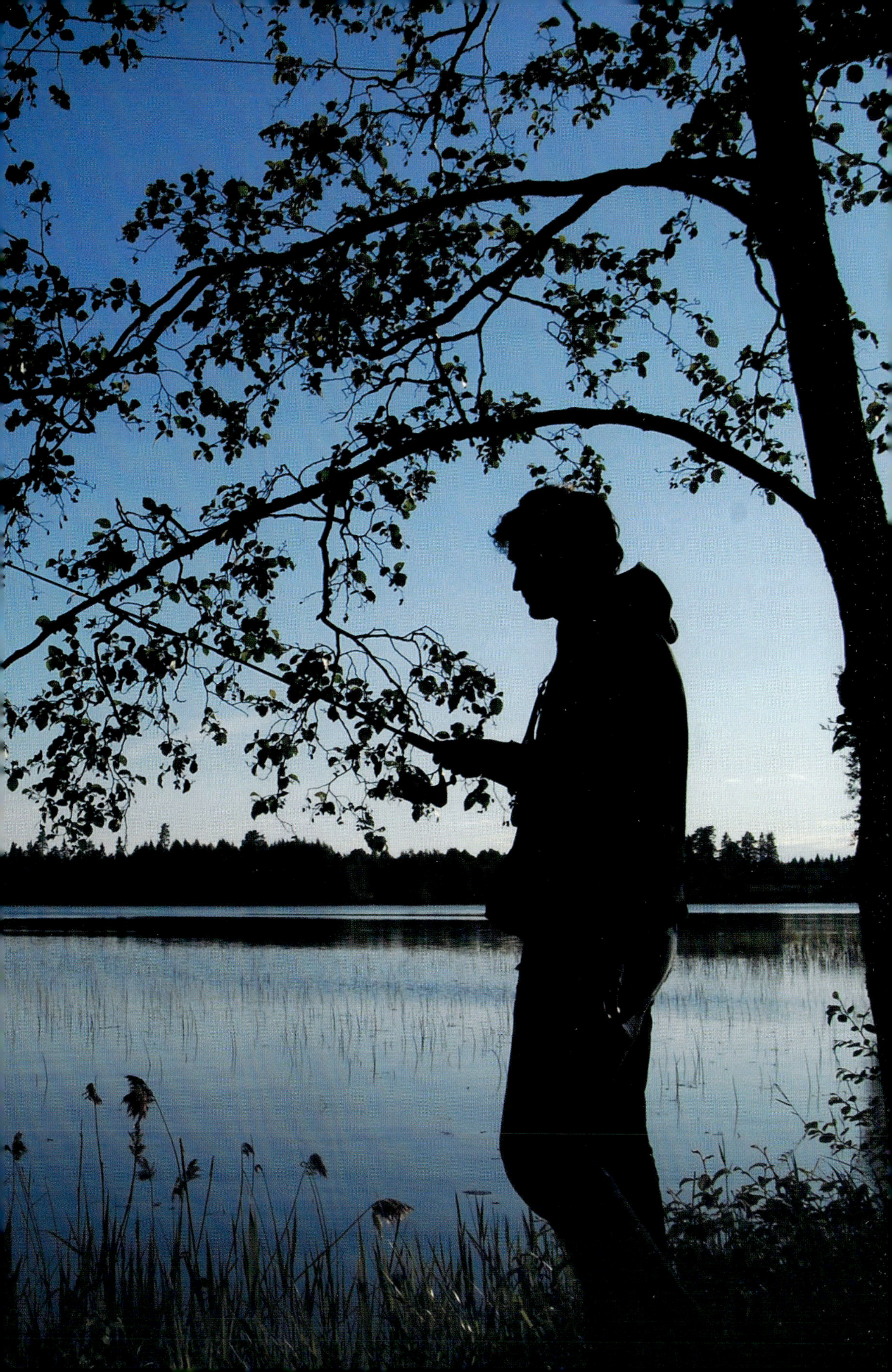

some craggy, obscure code. There must be two dozen waters within ten miles of our position and virtually every damned one of them is infested with roach, perch, bream, zander and yes, pike. An angler's wet dream.

With some 180,000 lakes to choose from, Finland is not exactly short on possibilities. You could spend a lifetime exploring, but the deserted ten acres or so of pine-shaded water before us seem a suitable enough place to start. I quickly tell my hosts that I'm going for a walk with a fishing rod. Very probably a long one.

Water laps against mossy rocks and the reed lines along a part-boggy, part-rocky shore which has absolutely no trace of human presence. I scan through the lure box for inspiration but sense that it probably doesn't matter a great deal what I select. Judging by looks alone, you might safely guess that no one has cast here in a very long time. Secluded is an understatement. For miles around there are no shops, no street lights, no traffic, no people—just woods and water.

The silver flash of a six-inch spoon is echoed by the flicker of darting roach in the clear margins. And so the game of walk and cast begins in earnest. Sweeping shots are aimed along the reedy edges, underarm lobs into dark, rocky holes, the spoon skipping across the waves before sinking with a flutter. With every turn of the reel the abrupt first knock of interest is anticipated, the distant rattle of a woodpecker the only distraction from the pulse and throb of the blade.

The cloud cut blue of the sky is vast and sleepy, the woods now dead still. Just as I wonder if the fish are further out in the deeps the rod tip bounces before dragging round hard. The line jolts into life and cuts rapidly back towards the rocks, spool clicking, carbon bucking. After thirty seconds of thrashing water and jagged power a first Finnish pike is steered within reach and I'm left still staggered at the raw power of this modest first catch, a lean and sinister thing of pine green and coppery gold.

Within half an hour the picnic weather darkens to a breezier, more troubled gray. But I'm not disheartened. Besides a few droplets of rain, a greater disturbance lingers over the water. Roach begin to flip clear along the bank. Reed stems knock, a menacing wake arrowing across the scene. Switching to a surface-popping plug I make a hasty move towards the crime scene. Could this lake get any more exciting?

After a hurried cast the plug spits and shuffles across the surface. Just as murder

The wonders of Finland (left to right): Home rolled lures, mozzie-geddon on the road, and a wandering reindeer just asking to get whacked dead by a passing truck.

"The word "take" seems inadequate to describe the explosion that takes place, an obscene blur of jaws and spray."

seems imminent I make one twitch too many and the attacker vaults clear out of the water, missing the plug completely. It hardly seems to matter. In fact, you half suspect that the near miss only serves to madden the pike, which takes the lure almost immediately on the next cast. The word "take" seems inadequate to describe the explosion that takes place, an obscene blur of jaws and spray. We are connected for a matter of seconds before the pike, a better one this time, cartwheels clean out of the water, the plug thrown clear in the opposite direction as I'm left statuesque, a jibbering idiot, hands shaking, wondering what happened, wondering where exactly I am and whether I 've stumbled upon the world's most beautifully primitive pike lake.

PERCH CENTRAL

I guess you'd call it a detour. A happy little accident. The little pool is spotted through a gap in some birch trees along a potholed mess of a road as I travel to a lake fifty times bigger. It starts with a narrow opening and an upturned rowing boat. The little bay beyond is no more than thirty yards wide, an army of trees giving way to a steep, rocky shore littered with mean looking snags. It's nearly irresistable. Call me flippant, but big adventures can always wait. The trouble is that a quick, cheeky cast soon becomes ten, twenty, and then a whole damned afternoon.

The float tube is already primed in the boot. I put on waders and flippers, backing quickly into the water and hoping the mosquitoes don't notice. It doesn't take long for my feet to stop clipping bottom debris and the depth to fall away. The lake looks like something out of a dinosaur movie, all dead things and damp remains. Anything is possible.

I kick a few paddled strokes out into the bay before taking aim with a spinner. This seems a sensible option given that I have no idea what fish exist here or even if this accidental lake has a name. On the first long, leisurely cast the spinner quickly bumps on something. A rock or stick perhaps? Next cast it happens again— a knock, and then another, bolder pluck on the line. This keeps happening until the little knocks are followed by a wriggling, shaking

Tangles with Pike   95

sensation. A cute, pint-sized and startled looking perch comes to hand.

The knocks continue with daft regularity. A small, bright yellow jig proves even more to the liking of the perch. On almost every cast they pluck at it like crazy. Occasionally they engulf the thing before I've even started reeling in. Sometimes a little gang of them follow the wiggly tailed lure almost to my feet, the whole group hypnotised like it's a primitive idol, no doubt the first lure they've ever seen.

All around are sunken branches, sinister lies. The snags just scream pike, but all I can find are perch. I try some bigger lures for a while—splashy mothers that dare something bigger to attack. But this draws a blank and I quickly get distracted and return to the undeniable fun of perch catching.

This goes on pretty much all afternoon as the perch keep biting and I keep casting, enjoying every pluck and throb and regressing to a mental age of about twelve. I try a new set of snags: perch! I try a deeper, rockier bank: perch! I go out further into the lake: perch! Most are small, all of them are fun, if a touch daft. Ok, make that totally naive.

For the first time in several days of exploring I also spot a fishing net besides a little lakeside cottage—hardly surprising given the Finns' love of perch as a tasty dish. I steer well clear of this dwelling and the hectic fishing continues.

It's mid-afternoon when, finally, the lure is snatched by something that feels considerably better. "Pike, surely this time!" I'm thinking. The fight suggests otherwise. It is a ponderous, meaty affair on my spinning rod, but not hectic enough to be a jack. After a few pleasing dives, up onto the surface rolls a broad, metallic flank. It is a golden, predatory ide. Resembling a cross between a chub and a large rudd, these creatures are fairly common in the lakes and take a small

"The trouble is that a quick, cheeky cast soon becomes ten, twenty, and then a whole damned afternoon."

lure or decent sized fly emphatically. It's not a pike, but the fish is a beautiful surprise. And it's not a perch.

I get just as excited when something gives a whack on the very next cast. It's another perch. And so it continues on a sunny, trigger-happy afternoon in the middle of nowhere as I assume the role of some sort of Pied Piper of perch fishers. After a lunch stop I then get a genius idea. In the corner of my lure box is a soft, perch-coloured jig, a bit bigger than the others. Surely, you might reason, any bigger predators here must have a taste for small perch?

Feeling clever I launch the perchy coloured lure along a rocky drop off, confident of success. For several minutes nothing happens, until right on the point of a little headland the line suddenly zips tight. Eureka! I play the fish carefully to hand and… it's another sodding perch. If nothing else the fish start to get slightly bigger including one or two beasts of all of half a pound. In the end I simply shrug my shoulders and keep perching. My hosts' pleas for fresh fish have been ignored so far but on this occasion I nab half a dozen or so decent samples for an evening fish fry. I'm already guessing they'll think I'm lying when I tell them I didn't catch a single pike.

LURED

By the time a week has passed the windscreen is a carnage of mosquitoes, a thousand black splatters, legs and wings. On a road running north towards nowhere in particular, stands a little fishing shack alongside a garage. Fuel, coffee and fishing is the general theme.

"The Silent People"—eerie Finnish art.

"This to catch metre long pike," I am informed in broken English… Finland is a country with fishing in its blood."

Consumerism is not exactly rife in Finland, I'm pleased to report. A bit of firewood, one or two guns, granted. Not a lot else. An entire wall of lures is nothing unusual in a Finnish tackle shop, but this place is less than conventional. Sitting amongst the Rapalas and Kuusamo spoons are row upon row of quirky wooden lures—not mass produced catchers but home rolled specials, lovingly carved and hand painted.

At one end of the rows are cute little plugs in roach and perch colours, while at the other end of the scale are foot long monstrosities in loud, blazing colours—surreal explosions of red, yellow and black. "This to catch metre long pike," I'm informed in broken English. Copper and silver spoons, flies and strange combinations of wood, metal and fur follow but this should come as no surprise because Finland is a country with fishing in its blood, where even a modest supermarket seems to have a thousand lures along with perch, trout, herrings and even smoked bream by the pound; where people are still intimately connected to the land and their endless waters.

More of my Euros are frittered away, unsurprisingly. The man behind the counter nods, sensing my devil-may-care enthusiasm. "We have basket if you want sir," he grins. "We also have trolley."

The array of oddities on display is nothing however, to the sight another hundred kilometres further North. "The Silent People" are around one thousand motionless figures, bearing random clothes and turf heads. A strange and eerie sight—but is it art? Or have

"The rod tip kicks gently once, twice, before the drag registers a slow, ominous click, click, click."

freezing winter temperatures rendered normal types of entertainment impossible? "Finland is about fishing and fornication," a Finnish angler once informed me, "and in the winter there is no fishing."

PANIC ON THE ROCKS

Line just keeps disappearing. Uncoiling and dropping, until we arrive at a sudden bump which signals the bottom. Is this any place for a solo voyage in a float tube? It is an eerie feeling to be paddling your way above a thirty-foot chasm, your feet hanging pathetically over a precipice. But in acres of shallow water such new found depths hold fresh promise.

One hundred yards further out lies an island, a stretched, rocky mass about half the length of a football pitch. An abandoned little summer house sits amidst the trees, half way between rustic charm and the last horror film you rented—patchwork roof, flaking boards, pile of wood plus rusty axe. Nothing stirs.

It's approaching the later part of the day, not that any true darkness will arrive at any stage. The sky smoulders burnt blues and oranges. It is now that we might find zander on the hunt, rising from their rocky sleep and terrorising the huge shoals of roach and vendace.

For a long stretch of time, casts are aimed at the island while I try not to think of the long paddle back to shore. In the stony, reedy edges the odd jack pike launches itself at a wobbling spoon or plug, but it is slightly further out that I get jitters of excitement. It is here, just as the lake bed sweeps down from painfully shallow to tantalisingly deep that I anticipate something better, a zander or a big pike I'm hoping.

The first dozen casts produce nothing but the odd graze of a rock. A black barred, silver Kuusamo spoon skips across the waves each delivery, weaving a few yards before flashing as it drops. For a good while there is no response. I think about moving on, but struggle to tear myself away from the island and the rocky corridor between stony beach and bottomless chasm.

It must be cast number twenty something when the lure stops. I think nothing of it. It won't budge. A boulder perhaps? A log the size of a corpse? The rod tip kicks gently once, twice, before the drag registers a slow, ominous click, click, click. I get that "oh shit" feeling. Click, click, click. The braided line gradually begins to shift away sideways as I steel myself for a fight, only half believing. The unseen weight begins to build, slowly shifting, the drag building from a thin ticking to a relentless spasm of panic. But it is only as the rod is flexed deeper that real offence is taken. The next few seconds are a frenzy of speed and bone jarring power, a ridiculous curve in the rod, the float tube itself rocking as the fish puts a gratuitous blur of yards between us. For a thrilling, terrifying minute about all I can do is paddle backwards and hang on, desperately holding whatever the hell I've hooked away from the rocky shore.

A momentary lull follows as the fish hangs deep and we both catch our breath. Total stalemate. I wind slowly and firmly, manoeuvring close to the fish before it takes offence again, flailing for the rocks. The weight is the same, but this time the run is less spirited and some sense of control quickly returns. With a beguiling ease the fish then comes in close, although still

Totally possessed: A manic, metre long pike.

too deep to steal a glance at. Steadily the gap closes until I'm almost directly above her. Another pause follows before the fish tries a different angle of escape—this time straight underneath me at speed, a wild rush that leaves me head down, the line grating between my feet, the rod wrestled from the vertical to sink down to the butt ring in lake water, more mad power.

It is indeed a pike. I don't know what else I expected, but the sight of a shovel head and a long, dark flank still stop the heart. The great fish now falters, and I grasp her under the chin. She's unhooked on the island shore. I have a no scales or sling but only the more portable means of a tape measure to settle on a number. Seconds later, well over a metre of fierce, dark Finnish pike slinks back into rocky depths.

It must be around eleven o'clock, but the sun hasn't set. Darkness will not arrive at any stage, the early hours lit by the strange glow of the midnight sun. I could happily sit here on the rocks all night, were it not for the mosquitoes. On the long paddle back to shore I try not to think about returning home and back to work, to the city, to the crowded streets of England. Aside from a new set of lures, all I have to show for the journey are pictures and tooth-marked fingers. Besides the mosquitoes, Finland has well and truly bitten me. ●

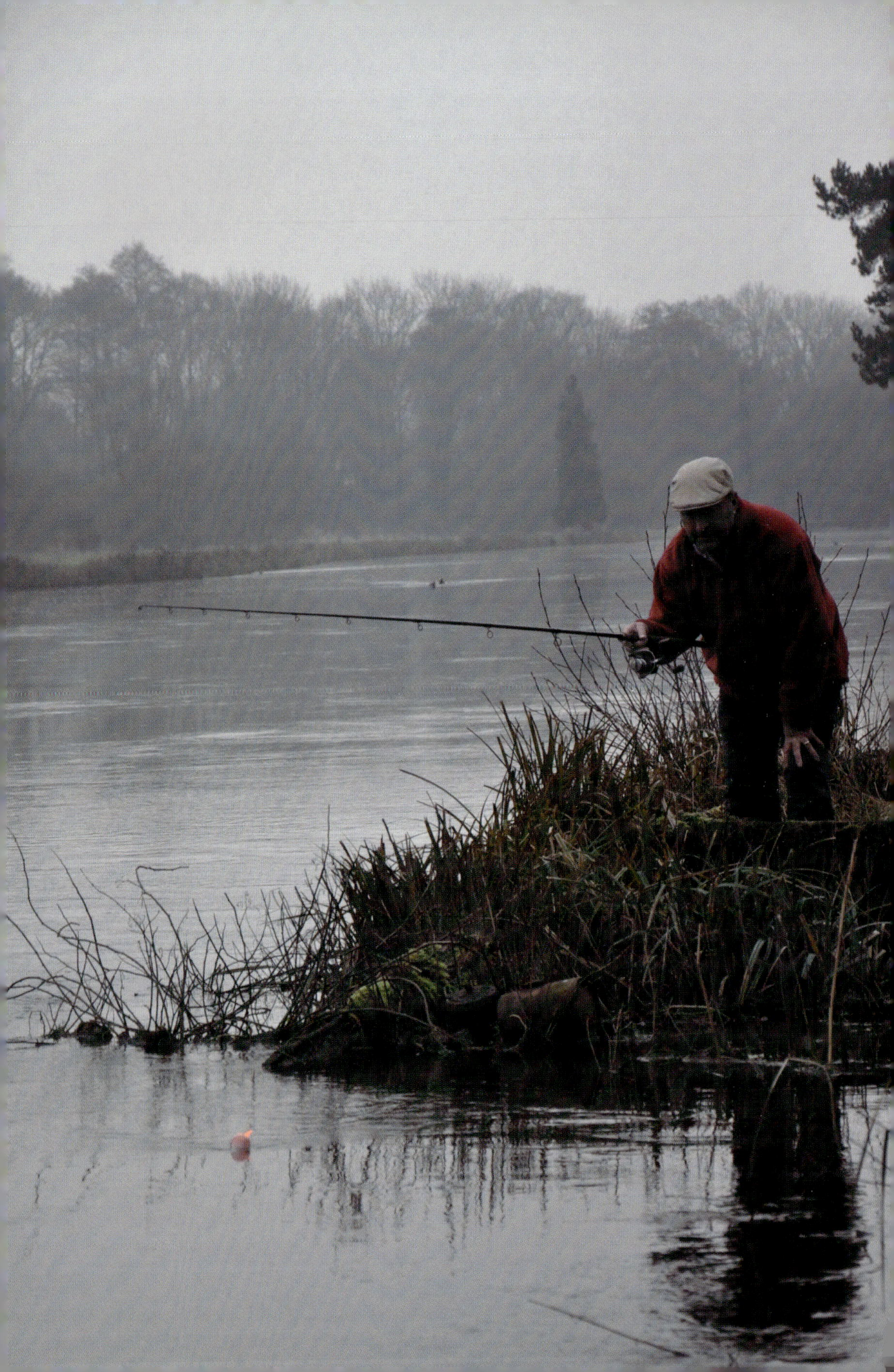

THE OPPORTUNIST PIKER

With over half a century of observations on running and still water Bob James has a keen eye and some fascinating thoughts on pike, as I discovered on the banks of the River Test.

Aside from the low, sulking temperatures and frosty fields, a typical chalk stream in winter doesn't necessarily strike you as a classic pike fishing scene. Then again, you wouldn't necessarily think of Bob James as a pike angler.

"I used to be really enthusiastic about pike fishing in the past," he says. "Nowadays I target them only at certain times or when guiding. I guess you could call me an opportunist piker."

Predator fishing is very much a minority sport on waters like the Test and Itchen. Even those beats where winter day tickets are available to coarse anglers, you don't see a great deal of pressure. And yet where left in peace, the pike are thriving. If these places have a history of culls and trout snobbery, things are slowly changing.

Bob has long been an advocate of game and coarse species living side by side. "I've never believed that pike are a serious threat to trout populations," he muses. "They're far more interested in roach and grayling shoals."

As facts rather than fiction about pike dawn on more river keepers, a healthier balance is being restored, at least in more enlightened quarters. Having kept an inquisitive eye on pike in many waters for decades, Bob is quick to point out their fragility, but also their ability to bounce back. "They just don't handle pressure," he laments, "which I suppose is part of the reason my piking has slowed down."

Tangles with Pike

THE OPPORTUNIST PIKER

Culls are another issue wherever game species are also present, but Bob often regards these as fairly pointless. "I've been amazed at just how quickly a lost pike is replaced," he comments. "You might get a bend on the river with a big old female, which somebody is desperate to remove. As soon as it's gone, another pike slightly lower down the pecking order will move into the same, prime spot and pack on weight in no time. A season or two later you'll find a fish that has reached similar size." Nor have pike always had such a low sporting or culinary value, he points out, and in fact at certain points of fishing history, they were more highly prized than salmon.

PIKE FISHING HIGHS
Say what you like about Bob, but his approach to any given species tends to be all his own, whether or not it agrees with the textbook. One of his biggest bones of contention with typical pike fishing is our assumption that we should present baits on the bottom. "So often with pike I think we assume they're glued to the river bed, so we actually place our baits beneath them," he remarks. "I catch a lot of fish on baits presented in mid water, or even higher in the water column. On many days, I've guided clients who've tried baits on the deck and yet caught twice as many fish with lures fished much shallower."

On the stretch of Test we find today, Bob enjoys casting lures, another method he really rates. This is another branch of fishing you might not associate with him, but after the success of "A Passion for Angling" Bob worked for Rapala and travelled far and wide casting lures. He has fond memories of the lakes of Finland, for example. "We visited the Rapala factory and tested all sorts of plugs across several large lakes," he recalls.

Trolling was never his favourite method, but this was exactly his task for an American fishing show visiting Scandinavia. "Anticipating some slower parts to the day I thought I'd surprise them," recalls Bob. "I had a whole box of lures without vanes and hooks, straight off the production line. We were out on this huge water and nothing was happening," he smiles. "I was that bored, so I grabbed a handful of plug bodies and threw them over the side. The Americans looked at me strangely and asked what on earth I was doing. 'I think you call this

> **"So often with pike I think we assume they're glued to the river bed, so we actually place our baits beneath them."**

chumming' I said. About a minute later, right on cue, my rod bent into a pike!"

Even further afield, Bob had an enjoyable time in America, discovering the world of competitive lure fishing. "They're absolutely crazy over there," he remarks. "The boats were incredible—to say nothing of the lures. Those anglers are ridiculously competitive in a way that's never taken off over here. I remember the pros would be making cast after cast at a frenetic pace for hours. Winning competitors were drug tested, and so the performance enhancers of choice were things like Mars bars, or 'candy bars' as the Americans call

With a mobile approach and often just one rod, Bob keeps his piking simple.

> "How can you not admire the pike? It's the most ancient fish we have. They've established their niche over millions of years. There's something perfect about a pike."

them, along with tins of coke. They'd carry bags rammed full of the things to keep their energy and concentration levels up."

Bob was later to win first place in a big competition day in the most unlikely fashion. "All the boats were hurtling off into Lake Texoma, which is a vast place," he remembers, "so I asked my boat partner if there was any rule against fishing from the bank, straight off the boat jetty." His American friend was mystified at this. Why would he want to do that when they had a state of the art boat at their disposal? The answer was simple. "I'd seen the end of the previous day's contest and noticed that all the big bass had been released right by the dock," smiles Bob. "I'd seen something similar in my match fishing days when fish put back would hang around for quite some time exactly where they'd been released." Casting his way around the jetty he caught several nice bass while the rest of the field were miles away studying fish finders. The only drawback was that the Yanks' new friend the crazy Englishman had to buy a lot of drinks that evening.

BACK TO BLIGHTY
As for Bob's exploits with pike in Britain, it's hard to know where to start. He had some great captures on the Hampshire Avon, where he also learned first hand just how quickly pike tales get distorted and rumors spread. "There was a stretch by an Inn that was especially productive. I'd fished behind an island and had a great day—with five fish all between mid doubles and nineteen pounds," he recalls. "By the time I went to the tackle shop a week or so later, the story had already spread and 'improved'!" he smiles. "The man on the counter asked me if I'd heard about the chap fishing the island who had five twenty pounders in a session."

Today, he's keen to explore the tail of a glide where he usually catches grayling. "When I'm trotting, I'd expect a pike to be sitting just downstream off the end of the shoal," he remarks. "Quite often you'll get a fish or two stolen here—and they certainly like to eat grayling."

He finds that the pike are seldom far from the bank. "I think it's a common mistake to cast for the far bank when piking," he says. "Somehow we always think the far bank looks more tempting than the one we're standing on. But often you're better off casting along the bank, and so many good fish seem to be within a couple of rod lengths."

His "accidental" encounters with pike have resulted in the discovery of some huge fish over the years. But does he really relish the appearance of the average jack wreaking havoc in his swim? "The amount of times on the chalkstreams pike have attacked my keepnet is crazy," he comments. "I've had several attacks on the same day and sometimes they literally get stuck by the teeth."

He has a big respect for pike however, even when his thoughts are on other species and they appear as gatecrashers. "How can you not admire the pike?" he asks. "It's the most ancient fish we have. They've established their niche over millions of years. There's something perfect about a pike."

It also strikes you that the idea of catching pike via the process of building a swim with

THE OPPORTUNIST PIKER

> "I'm tending to use trebles less and less... I went through a stage of hating them. Two trebles with bait or lures caused a hell of a mess with landing nets to say nothing of awkwardly hooked fish."

maggots is one few predator anglers exploit. There have been numerous occasions when a large pike gave itself away by nicking the roach or chub on Bob's hook. And while he admits not all of his pike were the original target he had in mind, his tally of three river thirties represents an impressive record for any angler!

His other theories on pike are also interesting, particularly when it comes to the back end of the season when the big ladies show up. Although it's a method he seldom uses these days, live baiting threw up some strange experiences in seasons gone by. "We'd try everything for some of these big pike, but they just weren't committed" he remarks. "It was as if you had to provoke them into a response that had little to do with feeding." On some days, a dace would be taken repeatedly in the strangest fashion: the pike would bite almost from sheer annoyance but never move off with the bait or turn on it properly, resulting in frustrating sport.

"I think pike occupy distinct areas," he states. "There are those where they feed, and those where they go to spawn. And that's why you find the fish in totally different spots in the late season." Could this also explain their weird behaviour around baits? "You have to ask whether these pike in spawning areas are really hungry? Or were they killing the baits because they were intruding on a territory, perhaps threatening to move in to eat eggs once the pike had spawned?"

Bob also spent long periods observing and prebaiting for pike with interesting results on other waters. Having baited up areas several times, Bob found the pike would often only play ball well into darkness. Such was the case at Wimbledon Park Lake, a shallow body of about twenty acres.

108   Tangles with Pike

"I was going morning noon and night, with sprats, herring, and mackerel," he remembers. "I also started tying baits to cotton to see where and when the pike preferred to take. Strangely, the colder the weather got, the later the pike wanted to feed. By January, there were times they only took baits at two or three in the morning, and were doing so in really shallow water."

CHANGING ATTITUDES

These days Bob confesses to a strong bias towards lure and fly fishing, methods he rates extremely highly. "Both lures and flies offer such a wonderful balance between efficiency and enjoyment." He believes these also signify progress in both tackle and technique. "Hooks have improved massively- and I'm tending to use trebles less and less,"

Tangles with Pike

THE OPPORTUNIST PIKER

> "If you value pike, and enjoy fishing for them, I think you have to consider what's good for the fish as well as what suits you."

he says. "I went through a stage of hating them. Two trebles with bait or lures caused a hell of a mess with landing nets to say nothing of awkwardly hooked fish—to the point where I thought I didn't want to put myself or the fish through that."

As far as Bob is concerned, his methods and piking in general have "evolved" to a large extent. "Soft lures or flies, with just a single hook are so much kinder than the plugs we once used—some of which had three trebles," he asserts. "By using single hooks as opposed to groups of trebles you're having comparatively minimal impact on the pike."

Bob is especially enthusiastic about these newer trends. "Soft lures have revolutionized both pike fishing and pike welfare," he says. "In many ways they're better for fishing. When we used big jointed plugs with large trebles, they'd rarely hit one twice because they're so hard and spiky. I've seen soft baits taken repeatedly—and I like just one single hook." He also likes the lower cost and versatility of such lures. "Not only are the soft lures great value, the much lower cost encourages you to be daring. You're less afraid of casting to snags, not only because they're cheaper, but because without hooks hanging off everywhere you're less likely to snag."

For Bob, it is attitudes that must change as well as tackle however. For too long, he believes, the mould for the British angler has been the out and out "trophy hunter", whose main aim is ruthlessly catching as many big pike as possible. You could argue that it is this size fixation that sees any "known" large pike being relentlessly pursued and recaptured until its demise. In contrast, he finds the 'sporting' attitude of the newer generation and particularly the Europeans and Americans healthier, whose ethos is "about having a good time, rather than just catching big fish."

110   Tangles with Pike

Bob cradles a chalkstream twenty. Thankfully many river keepers now take a more enlightened attitude to pike.

He identifies fly fishing as a continuation of this trend, as a method that is effective and hugely enjoyable, but also pike friendly when you consider the single hooks and avoidance of deep hooking.

The moral of the tale is therefore simple for our "accidental" pike enthusiast. "I think it's about meeting in the middle," he believes. "If you value pike, and enjoy fishing for them, I think you have to consider what's good for the fish as well as what suits you." Sometimes that means giving the pike a break, as well as adopting new techniques. It means enjoying our fishing and refining those methods that have less impact on pike, rather than aiming to chalk up specimen fish at all costs. And while Bob might have that annoying habit of catching more pike in "opportunist" fashion than many of us claim through slogging away at it, I think he makes a valid point. ●

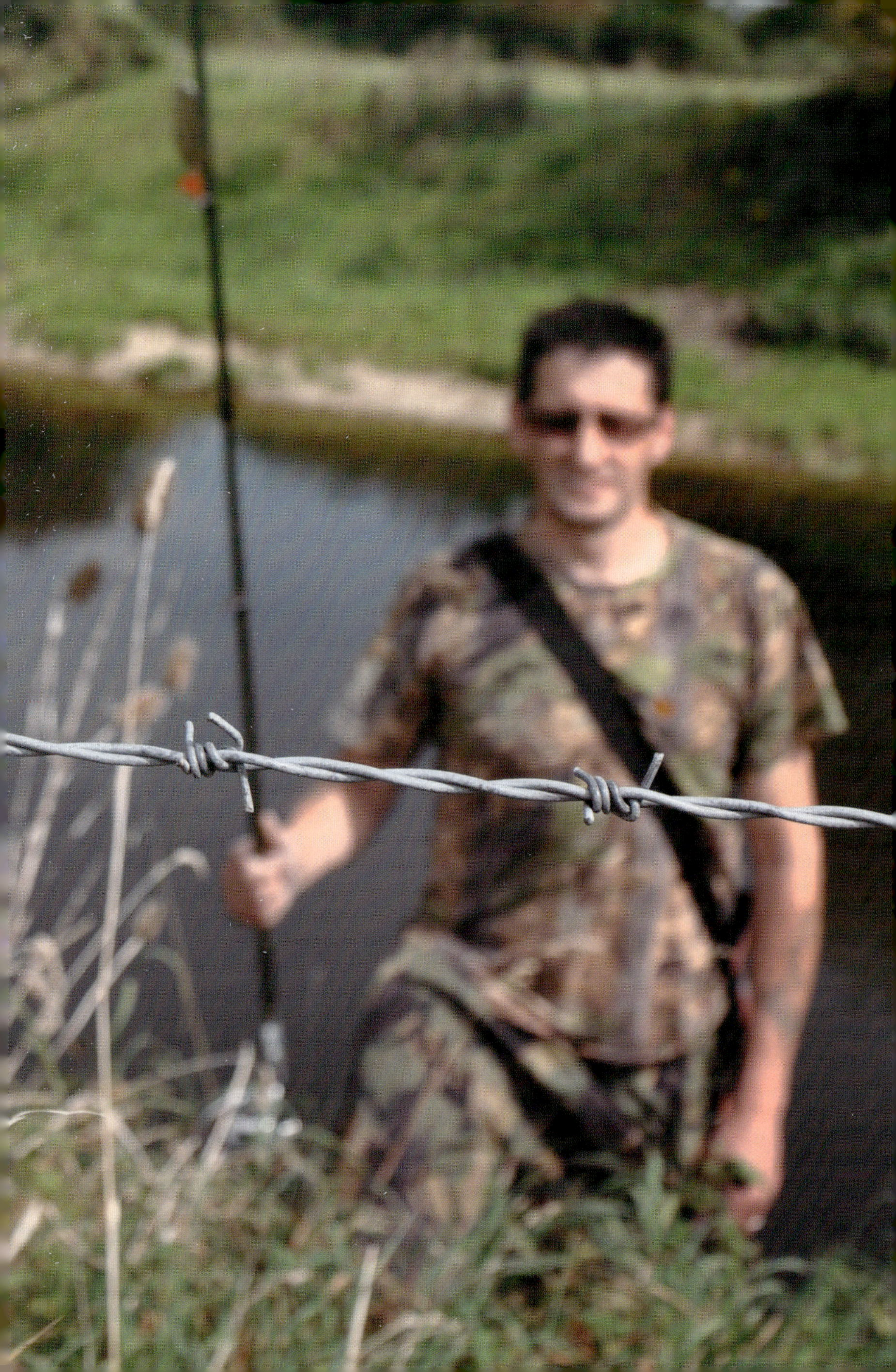

RIVER PIKE IN THE ROUGH

Braving nettles, barbed wire and antisocial hours, Nathan Edgell epitomizes the sport's restless, pioneering spirit.

If the world of modern fishing ever seemed a little tame, the perfect antidote would surely be a craggy river, littered with snags. Gone are the manicured swims, premium rate tickets and glossy brochures. Instead we enter a world of broken gates, brambles and mystery on a prehistoric scale.

On a shady reach of the Dorset Stour, I quickly find myself wondering where exactly Nathan Edgell is taking us. He scarcely bats an eyelid as we fend off vicious thorns and fight our way through oozing mud. It's like the bloody Lost World out here. It is this very taste for adventure, however, which has led Nathan to such phenomenal success with both his epic catches and much loved Adventures of a River Piker Facebook page. This season alone he has a string of awe-inspiring, totally wild fish. But before anyone gets too jealous, Nathan also has the stings, scratches and lack of sleep to prove it.

Judging by some of the feats accomplished, you might easily guess that this is a man with unlimited time, stacks of gear and access to named waters; and you'd be totally wrong. In place of that particular lucky sod, you're likely find someone a whole lot more familiar: a busy shift worker and family man in this case, armed with just a single rod and a restless, sometimes slightly manic passion for pike fishing.

Other surprises in Nathan's success quickly serve to smash any stereotypes and remind you what a gloriously simple sport pike fishing can be. Besides a relatively short career of just a decade or so of dedicated pike fishing, another nice surprise is the almost total absence of complex or costly gear. Finances are tight as a working dad, and virtually all of his recent captures were made on a budget £25 pike rod, which he uses for many different roles.

"Some pike fishing mates do like to comment on my gear," he grins. "I went to Chew with a very experienced angler who was quite embarrassed by having my kit on show. He kept telling me to hide the rod!" By the time you read this, the names of sponsors may well have crept into the equation, but part of me hopes not.

Armchair fishing it certainly isn't, as an invitation to have a "quick look" at a couple of swims leads us over hedges and through boggy ditches to find the really unfashionable bits of the river.

At times the pace of swim hopping is quite frenetic. If you ever thought you lacked patience when it comes to fishing, Nathan is in a different league. He is trigger happy, footloose and shows a healthy disregard for his own comfort or what the wife will say about the state of him when he gets home.

"Sitting still is just not in my nature," he says. "I'm always looking to cover water quickly and go and find the pike." His captures

Have rod, will travel: Nathan Edgell explores yet another lost river swim.

have come on a variety of methods, from lures to dead and live baits, but the one common denominator is his unerring will to search every corner—no matter how many branches poke you in the eye on the way in. Today's first swim is a point in case as we find a deliciously sinister looking slack at the end of a decidedly tangled route. Keeping well back from the water, he flicks a spoon out little more than two rod lengths out, before jinking it into life.

"The margins are so often the key area," he whispers. "Too often you see anglers make a long first cast, but I catch many of my best fish right by the bank within the first few minutes of arriving."

The next swim is hardly less gnarled. This time the fluttering spoon is battered at the first time of asking, as water explodes under the rod tip. With some fireworks at the surface but minimal fuss, a wildly marked jack is brought to hand. "Whatever the size of pike, I think it's better for the fish to play them in quickly," he says.

Another interesting feature of Nathan's approach is the use of single treble hook rigs for bait fishing. "Unless I'm fishing a stillwater with much larger baits, I always use just one treble,"

Tangles with Pike 115

he says. "Two hooks often just lead to more damage and more complication in my opinion." He insists on top quality unhooking tools also, which probably cost more than that rod! As well as a solid set of foot-long pike pliers, he is also never without sidecutters to remove awkward hooks. "Hooks can be easily replaced," he muses, "but you can't say the same about pike."

One area Nathan now does get some support from the tackle industry is with lures. He swears by the good old Abu Atom spoons for river fishing, but has also been field-testing jerkbaits and jointed plugs from one or two companies to great success.

As we proceed through what might politely be described as some pretty "rustic" swims,

"The big ones are great, but they're all good fun. I enjoy every fish, whether it's six or twenty six pounds."

you quickly see how lures suit his fishing style. "If I'm not catching I quickly move on," says Nathan, who also tends to fish the unholy hours of the day. Having a night shift job has helped him acclimatize to this, but his habits are as much about the necessity of bringing up two boys. The early hours when the family are asleep have often his only window of opportunity—although his boys are now also joining him to catch pike.

As we continue off the beaten track, more angry pike react to the lures. Today sees no new monsters, but they battle well in the current. "The big ones are great, but they're all good fun. I enjoy every fish, whether it's six or twenty six pounds," says Nathan.

Pondering my notes and looking through some of his pictures, I can't help but feel Nathan's story is a nice return to the basics that are so often lost in the many words about tackle and baits. The rules of engagement here are so simple, yet ring so true I'm tempted to have them tattooed to my body for reference: Be prepared to walk and get stuck in where others fear to tread; keep your tackle strong and simple; creep into position and never neglect the margins; pick the hours pike like to feed rather than those that suit a family stroll; take care of every fish you catch.

As we haul ourselves out of the rough and back towards the access point, wherever the devil we left it, I'm wondering if there is any other area of specimen fishing where such potential exists with such a modest outlay. How many top anglers would bank specimen carp or barbel with just one budget rod and some get up and go? This is the beauty of pike fishing, which Nathan sums up better than I could: "Anybody can get out there. You really don't have to be a name or have vast amounts of time or money to catch big pike." ●

WHERE THERE'S MUCK...

Grubby, tidal rivers are no place for the faint-hearted. But beyond the stench of salty mud is the possibility of a lunking, last-gasp pike.

You know the saying: "Where there's muck there's brass"? Well, in the case of my local tidal river, where there's muck there's rain, dead animals, despair, random debris and more muck.

According to closely guarded local sources, there's even the odd fish. If you can find them, that is, amidst that great soup which is the tidal Exe. Every day I spend on the banks the river follows a timeless cycle: the filthy water washes up, slides back down again, and I catch sweet Fanny Adams.

The last time I had a great big pike from these waters was approximately too long ago. Layers of muck have built up on my fishing gear since. I was relatively clean-shaven, at least if you could see my face beneath the mud. So where did the fish go? I blame myself partly. After all, I too plundered that handful of obvious, known spots. Can you blame the pike for not hanging around, or growing desperately cagey? Would the pigeons keep coming to the same spot in the park where local hoodlums were busy picking them off with an air rifle? To the fish it's about survival, not sport. You might get some tentative bites, the odd dropped run in last year's glory swim, but for me the answer isn't to get clever with rigs or sling extra rods out. No, it's time to leave them be for a while and take your rods somewhere else.

So why not somewhere well away from perhaps the stinkiest, muddiest river south of London? Well, for one thing I hate being beaten by a stupid fish of any description. But there's also the promise of something a little bit special, should you be prepared to get your hands dirty.

I have a theory as to why most anglers drive straight over the river and fish the ship canal. It's because it's friendlier to stroll and prettier to look at. All those lovely reed lines and overhanging trees simply breed confidence. You can already see the pike in your mind. Not so on the brackish sludge of the tidal where you might see just about anything, none of it very beautiful. This season's treats include a pneumatic drill and some poor bugger's shoes.

Me, lacking belief?

WHERE THERE'S MUCK

> When the going gets muddy, feeder rigs help overcome poor water clarity.

I've always been a sucker for a pretty looking swim, whether or not it's any good for fishing. Perhaps this is where I've been going wrong. A solid, brutish, mud-dwelling pike has no such tart's mindset and some of the ugliest areas are those with most promise. There's no shortage of space to hide and the more you study the river's length, the more you start to realize you've only just scratched the murky potential of its snag-littered slacks, deep channels and dank corners. But where there's a will, and possibly a long hike with a pair of waders, there's a way.

Plotting your attack involves keeping a close eye on conditions. If changeable weather and nomadic fish were not enough to worry about, the tide also brings its challenges. It's true that a pike might take at any time it finds an easy meal, but the bottom of the tide is a particularly interesting time to try. Perhaps at this stage, with lower flows and less water for their prey to hide in, the pike find it easier to launch their attacks? Having fired more blanks than John Wayne, I'm probably the last to expound a reliable theory.

Another valuable aid on such a forbidding, changeable water is to join forces with friends. Pike anglers are notorious for being secretive, grumpy types, but it needn't be so. Sharing information and ideas with a handful of trusted mates can be a big bonus, helping everyone in the long run. In my own case, it has been great to put heads together with Exe addict Chris Lambert, a man with this muddy river in his very blood. You can share your victories and defeats as you go, whether the text message starts with "Bloody slow again" or "You'll never guess what I just caught!" The latter message has been a long time coming in my case, unless you count the trip where I lost what looked like a specimen cormorant. The thing just materialized out of nowhere, but I digress.

Yes it's a muddy old task, the business of fishing on a tidal river. But it's funny how many

Worth getting filthy for; a tidal twenty from an obscure swim.

times you're rewarded just as you wonder what exactly you're doing conducting the filthiest offensive since the Battle of the Somme.

Such was the case last week. "One more crack" was the mantra at barely light o'clock. The water was running low and moody, looking more like a sewer than a classic river. A whole sardine on a feeder rig looked fairly bloody optimistic, tossed into a four-foot trench of water no more than three rod lengths out from the bank. I had already steeled myself for another long wait when, fifteen minutes into the session, the drop off indicator fell slack and line slipped into the murk at a steady pace. Striking early, I could tell this was no jack. The fish plunged deep and dirty, surging along the near side as the pressure grew between us. Grabbing the net I travelled down the bank half on my feet, half on my backside. The first glimpse made me shudder slightly—by god she was thick round the middle! Knowing all too well the perilous combination of a head shaking pike and barbless trebles, I resolved to sink the net early while saying a few obscene prayers. As my feet started to sink a little in the salty mud, she rolled once more before I enveloped her with the net. When the scales confirmed a fish just over twenty pounds, my pulse grew even more erratic.

So much for the waiting game then, with my late season monster fish arriving in one quick cast. But perhaps it's the many hours of grubby attrition that make that moment of connection so ludicrously thrilling, when the line pulls free of the clip, your heart wrenches and you remember why you hauled your semi-willing backside out of bed in the first place. For those few seconds of excitement-bordering-on-panic. For that fish that sulks low and determined. For that mad scramble down the bank, a creature thicker than your leg thrashing in the dirty water. Such a late season monster stays long in the memory. Sticks like mud, I'm tempted to say. ●

THE USUAL SUSPECT?

A solitary, lazy ambush predator, fearless to the point of stupidity, best sought out in cold conditions. We're all familiar with the stereotypes of pike and pike angling, but do these clichés really give us a helpful or accurate picture? Will the real *Esox Lucius* please step forward?

Take a few centuries of traditional assumption and add a dose of fear and ignorance. Grab a few healthy generalisations, throw in some outright bullshit and you soon start to realise that our knowledge of the pike is somewhat sketchy at best.

Perhaps we're just following a certain heritage. Izaak Walton, the godfather of fishing himself, thought that pike didn't breed at all but grew ominously from water weeds. Folklore simply assumed they were the work of Satan and in a curious way those cretins who still think "the only good pike is a dead one" are merely the next step in a chain of ignorance stretching back centuries.

Even in the relatively more enlightened times we live in, a whole series of lazy stereotypes about our old friend the pike have persisted. But what about the other generalisations still adhered to? And how exactly do you separate the gospel from the garbage?

"PIKE ARE STUPID AND FEARLESS"
Pike are fearless, reckless even. Mad, bad, scared of nothing and willing try to eat anything, at least, if you believe some of angling's big mouths. If there is one cliché that does no favours to pike or pike anglers, it is this idea of bold stupidity. Admittedly there is some ammunition there, because at times pike are simple to catch, just as there are times when carp, tench or most species are easy to trick. The difference is perhaps that the pike is not a fish that gently forages, but relies on swift attacks where the prey is taken whole. Most anglers will have a story or two about the pike that was caught twice in a day, myself included, and a hungry pike can sometimes be a reckless pike.

The bizarre and brash stories may grab the attention, but other more subtle observations and bare facts also need relating. I have seen pike spook at my presence on many occasions when looking into the margins. There surely can't be many coarse fish with better forward vision and I've seen them inspect, skirt around or even appear to spook directly away from baits casted into clear water.

Equally, there are many times when you receive twitches or tiny movements on the line which don't develop. Don some polarising glasses and you find that the culprits are not always eels but often pike, and some large ones to boot. I am currently in the process of fine-tuning my set ups for one such area, where the last four trips have resulted in several tiny twitches which never developed, along with two cagey takes that both resulted in double figure pike. "Gentle" is an understatement to describe some of the bites from this "fearless" predator. Is this the result of fishing pressure?

Of course, this opens another can of worms altogether, namely the whole issue of pike "wising up". The word "intelligence" is usually misapplied in this context, but pike have keen instincts and are superbly adaptable. A creature that has survived for many millions of years in such a wide range of habitats simply must be.

Far from being stupid or blindly aggressive, predatory animals are almost invariably more "intelligent" than other animals that share the same environment, displaying a far wider range of behaviours, and particularly "learned" behaviours. Fact. Think about it: which animal makes a more interesting pet, the cat or the mouse?

"PIKE ARE STATIC, AMBUSH PREDATORS"
You already know the time honoured portrait. Each pike has a "lair", lying in wait until prey comes close before rushing out to ambush it. It is a blueprint whose

Beautifully camouflaged yes, but the pike is not strictly an ambush predator.

general truth is borne out in the design of the species—its stealthy, powerful shape, camouflage and large head mark it out as a "one hit" ambush merchant.

This is a nice, uncomplicated picture that makes a convenient summary for nature reference books. Where it is less useful however, is in understanding the sheer variation in behaviour of this highly adaptable and unpredictable predator. Is the pike really so static? As many will testify, pike can and will travel a long way to position themselves close to prey shoals. Cover does not always equal pike, and prey movements are often a more reliable way of finding predators. I found the first hand testimony of BBC underwater filmmaker Dean Burman especially interesting in this regard: "When it needs to it will stalk" Dean told me about pike. "They will follow prey for hours and I've actually seen them swimming with the schools but not making any sharp movements until they strike. Another tactic they use is to lie on the floor and watch prey gliding over them."

An ambush merchant the pike certainly is—but when on the feed he can be a great deal more mobile than the traditional picture, meaning an active hunter as much as an ambusher. Clearly low light levels, early and late in the day or in gloomy conditions also afford *Esox* more licence to rove for food—and on big waters they may patrol great distances. Perhaps this is why overcast days are often far better than the bright, sunny afternoons beloved by fair-weather fishermen.

As for other feeding modes we know little. Scavenging behaviour, for example, is hardly documented and yet dead baiting is perhaps the staple tactic of the UK pike angler.

"PIKE ARE SOLITARY PREDATORS"

The pike is certainly not a shoal fish, and can be fiercely territorial too. So say the ecology books at least. Many also subscribe to the idea that large and smaller pike seldom mix outside spawning time, such is the power of their cannibal reputation. This seems a reasonable theory to some extent, although I'm inclined to believe that the cannibal tendencies of pike may have been over-

"The cannibal tendencies of pike may have been over-egged traditionally. Studies have shown that typically only a small fraction of the pike's diet comes from snacking on its smaller brethren."

egged traditionally. Studies have shown that typically only a small fraction of the pike's diet comes from snacking on its smaller brethren. The fascinating exception to this rule would be the occurrence of a few wild lakes around the globe where pike are the only major fish species. In such waters the very occasional big fish will be the jack eaters.

So given that pike have a reputation for avoiding each other, why is it that pike anglers will quite often find fish grouped together? Spawning clearly prompts pike to congregate tightly, but at other times too, you'll find pike clustered, usually in those areas where bait fish are grouped in numbers, indicating that they can be perfectly tolerant of other pike if food is abundant.

Perhaps then we should distinguish between the different areas we find the fish. There may often be "lairs" where fish will rest up but also feeding zones, the "dining area" if you like. How else can you explain all those times we enjoy multiple pike catches from relatively small areas?

There may even be times when attacking in numbers may benefit the pike. Far fetched? I'm not so sure. One situation comes clearly to mind. A pool I fish on a long, fairly featureless waterway has a large metal gate at one end. Roach gather in huge shoals here from late autumn onwards and consequently so do the pike—at first light I have witnessed several pike in the same area, smashing into prey close to the metal wall. It is almost as if they take it in

THE USUAL SUSPECT

> **"If we look at other top predators we find that they invariably pick on the weakest, most vulnerable and easily available prey, not necessarily the biggest."**

turns to clobber the fodder fish against a dead end (quite literally a "dead" end in this case). While none are tiny jacks, they are also a range of sizes.

"BIG PIKE PREFER A LARGE BAIT"

The "big bait for a big pike" argument has probably been raging since the very dawn of pike fishing. Initially it has a nice logic to it—bigger pike deliberately eat bigger fish, which provide more food than smaller prey. The science, however, doesn't necessarily lead to the same conclusion.

While it is certainly true that big pike can manage impressively large baits, this does not mean to say that selective feeding on large prey is their habit. I find it more believable that the pike is an opportunist who will take the easiest target every time. Observe a large shoal of roach and you'll inevitably see a minority of vulnerable individuals, fish with fungal patches or previous damage for example. Is the pike going to take the biggest fish in the shoal or the weakest?

If we look at other top line predators we find that they invariably pick on the weakest, most vulnerable and easily available prey, not necessarily the biggest. The young, the sick and the old are invariably most at risk (sounds a bit like society doesn't it?). Even if we entertain the idea that pike "choose" bigger prey, the truth is that although bigger prey items provide a bigger reward, they are also harder to subdue and more likely to lead to a wasted attack. In evolution successful predators are those whose behaviour leads to the optimum pay off—a case of food gained against the energy expended by catching it or attempting to catch it.

Undoubtedly, to thrive, pike ideally require a supply of various prey sizes. Are waters populated with mostly tiny roach therefore less likely to produce big pike? Those habitats where there are plenty of larger roach, bream and other species should certainly allow the pike population to reach greater size, with some individuals hitting the upper bracket. A fish of a pound or so is hardly a big mouthful for a pike of ten pounds or more.

Before I get lynched by the "my bait's bigger than yours" mob however, I would state that big baits are undoubtedly useful in the capture of pike of all sizes. A bigger bait is more visible, has more scent and creates more disturbance. This does not mean that big fish prefer big prey! A big pike will attack a small target, just as tiny jacks sometimes try to nail something large. Undoubtedly though, large baits get noticed more easily and are especially useful in coloured water or where vast areas must be searched. Which bait is more likely to be found, the sprat or the herring?

"PIKE FISHING IS BEST IN THE COLD"

A grand cliché if ever there was one. You'll still hear some old heads say it too: "What we need is a good frost". So where does our traditional pike season spring from?

Perhaps the most glaring reason is that traditionally the British angler spent the warmer months fishing for roach, tench and

THE USUAL SUSPECT

Pike have an eye for an easy kill, but not necessarily the biggest meal available.

other species, whereas in the dead of winter, pike were still a viable target when the going was tough. The dying back of weed growth and clear, cold water can make life tough for predators and so consequently they were thought to be more likely to accept a free meal, even one of dubious origins.

The theory sounds good at least, and there is nothing wrong with tradition and the romance and ritual of winter piking. But today's pike angler is more likely than ever to fish right through summer, or at least outside the traditional season and let's face it, the pike still often feed readily. I know anglers who have taken some huge pike in the summer, despite the text books saying they "disappear" at these times. Being cold-blooded, they are often going to be more active in milder temperatures, perhaps with the exception of really warm, oxygen deficient water.

But naturally, catch rates are a secondary consideration to many of us when pike welfare is at stake and the colder months undoubtedly offer released pike a far greater

Tangles with Pike

THE USUAL SUSPECT

> "At this moment the fishing writer gives an awkward pause. Because in truth, the fascination and frustration of the whole game is that pike are as varied in their habits as the sheer variety of waters we find them in. This is one investigation that could last a lifetime."

chance of full recovery. For bigger pike especially, summer can be a time of stress and evidence suggests that better pike waters require deeper, cold water areas for mid summer. My own occasional forays in hot weather are now almost always taken on large, deep lakes or rivers with reasonable flow—a guarantee of decent oxygen levels and cooler temperatures. And yes, I have seen pike die in the summer after being caught, even with careful handling, which is why I refuse to target them in warm water these days.

Perhaps the only conclusion we can draw to this debate is that settled weather is usually more productive than extremes of hot or cold—with the start of a new weather pattern such as a cold snap especially likely to trigger activity. It is also said that *Esox* is a "cold water species" by nature. Certainly you find that in other countries, for example, warm shallow lakes can be devoid of larger pike. On the other hand though, any species that can thrive in habitats from the balmy Deep South of the USA through to the bitter winters of Scandinavia must be pretty versatile.

THE TRUTH IS OUT THERE SOMEWHERE...

In this bizarre world we live in, popular myth and science live in an uneasy coexistence. Fishing is also a great sport for those pub theorists who will enthusiastically support the most unlikely truths and dubious claims. Quite frankly the world would be a duller place without these characters. But any serious pike angler knows that the species are rarely as predictable as we'd like them to be.

Successful anglers are successful observers, who are able to respond to what is in front of them rather than taking their cue from the same, rather general advice dragged out every season... and at this moment the fishing writer gives an awkward pause. Because in truth, the fascination and frustration of the whole game is that pike are as varied in their habits as the sheer variety of waters we find them in. This is one investigation that could last a lifetime. ●

MORE FROM DOMINIC GARNETT

FLYFISHING FOR COARSE FISH (MERLIN UNWIN BOOKS): The convention-busting book that became an Amazon Bestseller. Hailed as a modern classic, it details tactics, techniques, flies and novel ideas on all the major coarse species in a lively, absorbing style.

"The most original, fascinating and eye-opening fishing book I've read in years." Scottish Sun

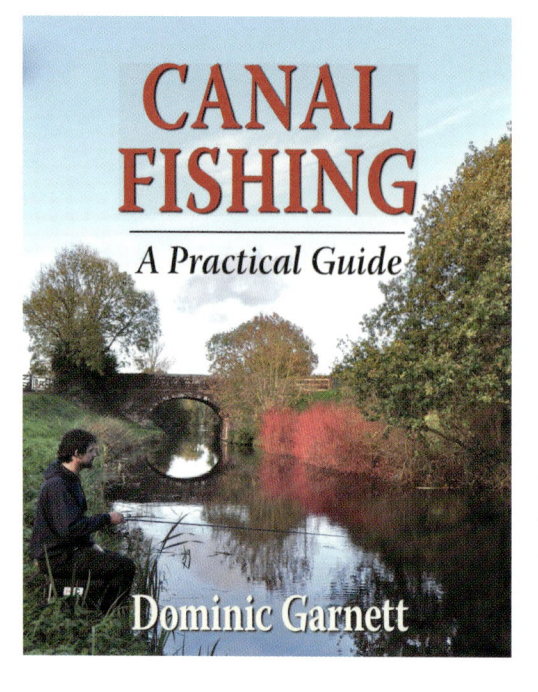

CANAL FISHING: A PRACTICAL GUIDE (MERLIN UNWIN BOOKS): With hundreds of miles of untapped fishing, canals offer a huge range of exciting, affordable sport. This beautifully illustrated volume opens up a world of species, methods and possibilities, as well as an extensive guide to UK canal venues, including both local and national specimen fish records.

FISHING FOR DUMMIES UK EDITION (WILEY & SONS): An entertaining and user-friendly introduction to coarse, fly and sea fishing in the UK. Perfect for beginners and those returning to the sport.

"One of the most readable angling writers in the business."
Angling Times

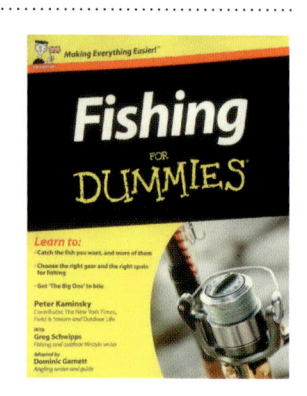

MORE FROM DOMINIC GARNETT

FALLON'S ANGLER: Featuring great stories from the likes of Chris Yates and Tom Fort besides the author, this beautifully presented quarterly represents the best in original angling writing: **www.fallonsangler.net**

PIKE ANGLERS CLUB OF GREAT BRITAIN: Working towards pike conservation and a more enlightened attitude to the species, this organisation is one for any keen pike angler to join. Their website also has essential advice on safe practise and catch and release guidlines:
www.pikeanglersclub.co.uk

DG FISHING: The author's website includes further words, photography and a range of brilliant flies, books, prints and gifts, as well as his regular blog "Crooked Lines".
www.dgfishing.co.uk

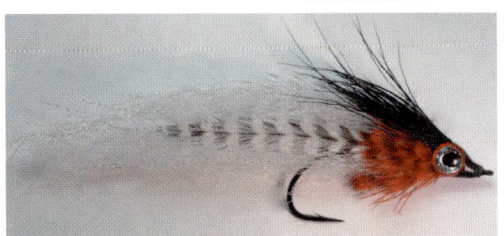

Tangles with Pike   131

www.dgfishing.co.uk